WHAT TURNS US ON

IRIS AND
STEVEN FINZ

WHAT

TURNS

US

ON

REAL PEOPLE CONFESS

THEIR MOST INTIMATE

AND OUTRAGEOUS

SEXUAL FANTASIES

ST. MARTIN'S PRESS ❧ NEW YORK

A THOMAS DUNNE BOOK.
AN IMPRINT OF ST. MARTIN'S PRESS.

DESIGN BY SONGHEE KIM

ISBN 0-312-14758-9

TO ALL WHO CONTRIBUTED TO

THIS BOOK BY SHARING THEIR

MOST INTIMATE SECRETS WITH

US AND OUR READERS. AND ES-

PECIALLY TO . . . (WE PROMISED

NOT TO MENTION YOUR NAME,

BUT YOU KNOW WHO YOU ARE).

CONTENTS

WHAT TURNS US ON

INTRODUCTION

"TELL US WHAT TURNS YOU ON. TELL US YOUR MOST INTI-
mate secrets so that we can tell the world." Maybe that doesn't sound
like the best possible way to start conversations with strangers, but as
this book demonstrates, it worked remarkably well for us.

Many psychologists and sociologists spend their entire professional
careers trying to determine why the things that turn people on, turn people on. They write books chalking up the specifics of arousal to childhood experiences and deeply buried memories. A man who is aroused
by the sight of a woman's high-heeled shoes, some experts believe, may
be remembering something that happened when he saw his first pair of
them as an infant. A woman who fantasizes about huge penises may have
been influenced by the sight of a naked man at a time in her childhood
when everything about grown-ups seemed incredibly large.

Books such as these make fascinating reading, but have not really
helped us understand our sexuality. Instead, our most useful knowledge
has come from conversations with people who were willing to talk
about their own thoughts and experiences. We've met and interviewed
hundreds of subjects. It's what we do for a living.

At first, the people we interview speak in stilted clinical language, trying to give us the answers they think we expect. They use terms read in

pop-psych books or heard on television talk shows. Yet, when they find out we're just ordinary people writing about ordinary people *for* ordinary people, their affectations drop and they begin to open up.

For us, it all started thirty years ago, when we were writing erotic fiction to finance our education. Our friends found this intriguing. They asked us how other people acted in the bedroom and revealed their own sexual behavior. We used information from one person to answer questions from another, until pretty soon we started feeling like a clearing house for sexual data.

Eventually, we collected enough stories to fill a book about the fantasies that couples enact in their most intimate moments. We wrote that book and called it *Whispered Secrets: The Couple's Guide to Erotic Fantasy* (NAL Dutton, 1990). Soon readers began getting in touch with us to tell their own stories. We gathered so many recollections of favorite erotic experiences that we filled another book, *The Best Sex I Ever Had: Real People Recall Their Most Erotic Experiences* (St. Martin's Press, 1992).

After the publication of our second book, we heard from journalists and broadcasters all over the world. We appeared on dozens of radio and TV shows, talking about the interviews we had conducted. In response to this publicity, we received hundreds of letters and phone calls from listeners, viewers, and readers of our books. As usual, some people had secrets to reveal, while others had questions to ask. And the one question they asked most frequently was, "What turns people on?"

At first, we thought mere curiosity prompted the query. Gradually, however, we came to realize that lots of folks feel guilty about the things that excite them and seek validation of some kind—evidence that their sexual interests aren't perverted or unusual. Perhaps, their guilt arises because our society tends to forbid discussion of sex, which prevents people from knowing about any sexuality but their own.

Most of the time, we were able to tell people that others found the same fantasies or experiences to be sexually exciting. Somehow, this knowledge made our questioners feel better—made them realize that their own secret thoughts might not be so unhealthy after all. We felt good about being able to reassure them and decided to work on a larger scale. In our interviews, we began asking people to tell us specifically about their favorite turn-ons.

Some of our subjects were young, having begun to explore their sexuality only recently. Others were older, with years of experimentation behind them. The one thing they had in common was their willingness to talk to us. We let them know from the start that we weren't taking a survey. We made no attempt to reach a random sample, and we have no statistics to offer about what percentage of people have which preferences. Frankly, we are suspicious of surveys because we don't believe that they accurately record information about a random sample, or that a random sample even can be found.

We are not doctors or sociologists or psychologists or any other kind of "ologists." We don't try to analyze or explain why people feel the way they do. We aren't offering treatment or diagnosis. All we do is listen and report. People tell us about their lives, and we write what they say the way they said it. There aren't enough pages to tell all the stories we heard or to describe all the things that turn people on, so we selected eleven common themes and picked several strong illustrations of each. We tried to write in the language of our informants, taking editorial liberties only for the sake of clarity or to protect the anonymity of our contributors.

We realize, of course, that people don't necessarily do the things they like to think about doing, so it is possible that some of the experiences described to us never really happened at all. We have made no attempt to verify the truth of the stories we were told because we are interested in learning what people believe about sex. Even fantasies reveal the thoughts of those who describe them.

When friends ask what our book is about, we keep the explanation as simple as the title. It's about what turns people on. We hope you enjoy it. Moreover, we hope that, by looking at the sexual attitudes and activities of others, you will learn something about your own.

1
I'LL TAKE ROMANCE

THE WORLD MAY BE CHANGING FAST, BUT THERE ARE SOME traditions that never die. When we asked people to tell us what turns them on the most, the answer we received more than any other was romance. We heard it from people of all ages, married as well as single. Men said it just as frequently as women.

When people speak of romance as a sexual turn-on, however, no two of them mean quite the same thing. All agree that romance has something to do with feelings of love and that these feelings are what lead us to arousal. From that point on, though, the descriptions go in very different directions.

Many prefer an arousal that builds slowly, during quiet evenings at home with a beloved mate. One person we interviewed said that for him and his spouse, true romance was sitting together on the sofa, holding hands, while watching a favorite television program. Another talked about candlelit dinners and soft music on the stereo. For both, the serenity and security of comfortable surroundings evoked feelings of tenderness that led to kisses and caresses which stretched out over a period of hours before blossoming into full-blown sexual excitement.

For others, romance involves a sudden jolt of overpowering desire. Such people crave an adventure that will carry them as far as possible from everyday life. They picture themselves falling hopelessly in love at the first sight of an exotic stranger in a magical setting. One woman told us that she experiences a rush of erotic excitement when she imagines meeting her dream-partner on a Mediterranean cruise or an African safari. A young man confessed that he frequently masturbates to a fantasy about a vaguely unique sexual experience he will someday have with a glamorous sloe-eyed woman who will speak in a husky voice with an unidentifiable and mysterious accent.

There are some for whom romance has nothing at all to do with setting or background, but is instead wedded to the notions of emotional generosity, self-sacrifice, and consideration for a partner. For such people, a gift might be regarded as romantic, not because of its cost or intrinsic value, but because the giver went to a great deal of trouble to obtain it. A man we met, for example, spoke tearfully of the year his girlfriend presented him with the issue of his hometown newspaper containing the announcement of his birth. Similarly, a woman told us that the most romantic thing ever to happen to her was when her husband wrote her a love poem on their fortieth anniversary and framed it, along with ticket stubs from the play they had gone to on their very first date.

The frequency with which people referred to romance as their greatest turn-on made it easy for us to select this as the book's first chapter, but the diversity of experiences described made it difficult to pick the examples to be included. After much deliberation, we have selected two that we feel demonstrate both ends of the spectrum.

Vikki's romance died, but was born again. Her story is about a love resilient enough to overcome a full-frontal attack, finding renewed life in a fragrantly exotic setting. Arno's tale is not about love, but about falling in love. For him, romance is a spark that lights his existence for a brief moment before sputtering and fizzling out, forcing him to look for it time after time.

RECONCILIATION

Vikki, who just turned forty-five, is personable and easy to talk to. Her long black hair and graceful figure combine to give her a quiet beauty. Her oval face is ex-

*pressive, with hazel eyes and pouting red lips. She looks wistful when she says
that romance is what turns her on the most.*

You'd be surprised how a romantic place, a romantic setting, a romantic
mood can change the way you feel about life. It worked for Hank and
me. Without romance, our marriage fell apart. And romance was the
only thing that could save it.

Hank and I had been married for fifteen years when the trouble
started. He was going through some kind of a midlife crisis, I guess.
There was a war raging inside him, and our sex life was the first casu-
alty. I felt it right away.

Sex between us had always been soft and tender, a real expression
of our love. An air of romance saturated our bedroom. Every time he
touched me, it felt like the first time. Every time he kissed me, I got that
same thrill I got when we first fell in love.

Then, suddenly, the romance was gone. We weren't making love anymore. We were just having sex. Without romance, sex seemed pointless and mechanical. We had orgasms, but no real fulfillment.

One day, Hank astonished me by announcing that he wanted
out. He said he needed to be free: free of emotional obligations, free to
make his own choices, free to do the things younger men do when they
are first learning about life. He wanted to be single, so I agreed to a divorce.

I've learned that in every divorce there's one person who feels the
pain more than the other. In ours, it was me. I had not fallen out of love
with Hank, and I had not really wanted the divorce. I was miserable. I
didn't feel whole without Hank. I felt that half of me was missing.

Hank was the only sexual partner I had ever had, and I did not want
another. I had always thought that we were perfectly compatible. Apparently, Hank did not. I wondered what I had once that I didn't have
anymore. Life seemed to have swallowed me up. Without any explanation or reason, my wonderful world of love and romance had suddenly crumbled. I felt like a stranger in a strange and ugly land.

To complete my frustration, I had no sexual outlet. The sense of romance in our life had always made sex wonderful between Hank and

me. We had genuinely enjoyed giving one another pleasure and fulfill-ment. Sexually, we had done everything either of us could think of. Everything had turned us on because our romance had kept us fasci-nated with each other.

Before long, I heard that Hank was dating one woman after another. My friends were running into him and his new partners all over town— in a five-star restaurant, at a taco stand, in a movie theater, in a cock-tail lounge. He turned up in dozens of places with dozens of different women, all of whom were young, good-looking, and chic, according to the reports.

At first, in a very strange way, I was almost glad to hear of Hank's flamboyant behavior because it seemed like only a fling. Even though our divorce was final, I thought he might come back to me as soon as he burned himself out on his quest for the fountain of youth. But after a while, his actions made me furious. There I was still grieving over our broken marriage, barely existing in a dull drab colorless world, while Hank was savoring the sweet scent of romance.

I decided that sauce for the gander could be sauce for the goose. I started dating, too. I joined a couple of clubs and told all my friends that I was on the lookout for interesting men. I went out a few times, but it just didn't work for me. Nobody I met understood my desire for romance. All they wanted was to jump into bed, which I just couldn't do.

I needed sexual fulfillment, but I couldn't sleep with some guy for sex alone. Sex wasn't enough. I needed to be loved. I needed to make love. I couldn't imagine being loved by anybody but Hank.

I didn't understand how it could be so easy for him to find romance with other women. I thought the trouble might be with me. Maybe I had gotten old, used-up, unattractive. I started jogging, swimming, and working out at the gym four to five times a week. I felt physically bet-ter, but emotionally, I was totally without hope.

Everyone I knew told me that the suffering would ease, but my pain did not dwindle. It just gnawed away inside me. I accepted that I'd al-ways be alone. I wasn't interested in trying to find a new partner. I didn't believe I ever could, or would, and I didn't even want to. If I couldn't live with Hank, I wouldn't live with anyone.

Then, three years after the divorce became final, Hank called me. I couldn't believe my ears. By then, communication between us had become almost extinct. I expected him to say something that would hurt me even more, but to my surprise, he started begging my forgiveness.

He said he knew he had made the worst mistake of his life when he walked out of mine. He said it took time and other women to make him realize just what he had with me and all that he lost when he left. He said he wanted us to try to get together again, if it wasn't too late. His voice was so filled with pain that I knew he meant what he was saying. There was even something romantic about it.

Not right away, but soon after that, I agreed to give our relationship another try. At first, we took things real slow. We continued to live separately. We dated like we did when we were younger. We'd go out to a movie or to dinner. Then, we returned to separate homes.

We had sex, but it wasn't like before. It didn't feel natural, and there wasn't any real romance involved. We didn't talk about the difference, but Hank was aware of it, too. I think we both knew that we would have to find some way to recapture the old magic.

One night, when Hank came to pick me up for dinner, his face was shining with enthusiasm. He said he had just learned about a spectacular resort, designed especially for loving couples. He asked me to go there with him for a holiday that would put the romance back in our relationship. I agreed immediately. A couple of days later the arrangements were made, and off we flew.

My description won't do justice to this hideaway among the Hawaiian Islands. Everything was geared for romantic enchantment. The island was remote and relatively unknown, as if God had created it just for our reunion. We had to fly there from Oahu in a small chartered plane.

The tiny isolated environment was completely surrounded by blue water clear enough to let us see everything that lived in it, right down to the very bottom. Stately palm trees swayed gracefully in the warm refreshing wind, and beautiful flowers were everywhere, in a variety of splashy colors. Their perfume was intoxicating.

The island boasted only ten guest cottages, but had enough servants to take care of a person's every possible want or need. If you had requested service, you'd never have to lift a finger. Someone would always be on hand to replenish a glass, or fill a plate, or turn down the bed.

When Hank booked our stay, however, he had requested privacy. We still received all the service we wanted, but the staff came only when we beckoned by pushing one of the many call buttons located in our quarters. Although we knew there were other people at the resort, we never saw any of them.

Our hut, as the management called it, had a rustic thatched roof, but an elegant interior containing a large bedroom with a king-sized bed, a smaller sitting room, and a dining area with a complete wet bar. Outside, a double-sized hammock and our own hot tub faced the ocean. On a large patio table sat a huge platter, always filled with exotic fruit grown on the surrounding islands.

Hank couldn't have picked a better setting for our reconciliation. It was a perfect place for us to be alone and get to know each other all over again. I was enthralled by our surroundings and the aura of romance that filled the air. It made me feel wonderfully alive again. I wanted to make love there.

Soon after we arrived, Hank and I were lying together in the hammock, gazing up at the clear blue sky, when we noticed an array of colorful exotic birds perched on a nearby palm tree. Two of them were rubbing their heads and beaks together. "Look," Hank said. "They're kissing."

With that, he took me in his arms and pressed his lips to mine. We kissed for a long time, alternating between fiery passion and delicate tenderness. I felt Hank's love coming through to me as it did so long ago.

The kiss warmed us both, until our hands began roaming over each other's bodies. The weather was gloriously warm and neither of us wore very much. All Hank had on was a pair of shorts, and I somehow managed to get them off him. The top of my brief bathing suit fell away without any help from either of us.

I had never before been bare-breasted outdoors. The sunlight stroked me with its heat as Hank began caressing me with his fingers and lips. Before our marriage went sour, he had touched and kissed my breasts for hours. I had missed his loving attention so much that when he kissed my nipples, I felt a burning need to have him inside me.

My bikini bottom fell to the ground as I wriggled out of it and wrapped my thighs around Hank. His hunger was as strong as mine. His manhood found me unassisted, and he entered with one smooth thrust.

We pressed our bodies together, feeling the hammock sway gently as we moved. We adapted ourselves to its rhythm. The motion, the soft ocean breeze, and the warm tropical air all contributed to bring our lovemaking to completion within moments. We climaxed together gently, experiencing sex as a true act of love.

Afterwards, we swam while waiters prepared an exquisite arrangement of tropical delicacies and native specialties. We dined as the sun set. Then we relaxed with cordials in the purple twilight, listening to the strains of soft flowing music played by unseen musicians.

The evening darkened gradually and then began to brighten as a brilliant full moon rose behind us. Its pale illumination reflected on the waves, turning the sea into a shimmering field of diamonds. Hank took my hand in his, and we slowly strolled along the beach at the edge of the ocean. We were like Adam and Eve, placed in paradise to start a new life together.

Hank said things I had thought never to hear again. He spoke of his love for me and said he knew he never wanted to be without me. He stroked my hair and kissed my throat and held my hand tightly in his. "I want to make love to you," he said. "Right here on the beach under the moonlight."

I felt a rush of passion. Everything felt so good, so right, so absolutely perfect. We embraced as we sank slowly to a soft bed on the shining sand. Only the moon was witness to the frantic urgency with which we tore at each other's clothes and clutched at each other's bodies. Hank pressed me down on my back and began kissing me everywhere, starting at the soles of my feet.

He sucked gently on my toes before moving his lips slowly up the length of one leg and back down the other. He stroked my belly with his lips and pressed his cheek to my navel. He gently kissed the undersides of my breasts, running his tongue along the creases where they meet my chest. He was slow and thorough, careful not to leave any space on my body unloved. He took each of my nipples in his mouth and brought them to peaks of erection by sucking lightly at their swelling tips, taking his time to please me by doing all the things he knew I loved.

It was delightful to be naked in the warm night air, to feel it gently exploring my sensitive skin. When Hank cupped my breasts in his hands, I sobbed with desire. We weren't just having sex, we were making love again.

I reached for the comforting strength of his masculine body, running my fingertips over the muscles of his thighs and buttocks. "I love you," he whispered as he poised his body over mine. "You look so beautiful that the moon must be proud to shine on you. I'm glad you waited for me. I now know how lucky I am to have you."

His words moistened my eyes and the hungry place between my legs. I spread my thighs to invite his entry, lifting my ankles in the air to point my feet at the starry heavens. He knelt before me, his erection seeking its proper home in the warmth of my love for him.

I flowered open for him as he nudged gently, seeking admission. Then, almost imperceptibly, we became one. The warm flesh inside me closed around him, and I was exquisitely aware that our bodies were in total union. It felt perfect, as though the opening in my body had been custom-made to receive his thrust.

When he had penetrated me to the limit, we lay still, as if our bodies needed time to relearn the wonder we once had taken so much for granted. I tensed the muscles of my groin, my vulva telling his penis how good it was to have him back. We pressed our groins together, then moved slowly apart in an erotic ballet in the sand. His penis stroked the inside of my vagina, which contracted hungrily with each of his driving thrusts. We moved that way for a long time, using sexual contact to communicate our love.

The air around us was filled with the fragrance of romance and a million brightly colored flowers pouring forth their perfume. The gentle lapping rhythm of the ocean's waves against the smooth white sand and the soft swishing of the palms in the warm evening breeze played an exotic serenade. Muted rays of the moon bathed the night in an eerie mystic light.

We merged with our surroundings as our bodies fused with each other. We climaxed simultaneously in a thundering flash, but the ecstasy went on forever. Our beautiful surroundings provided a fitting backdrop for our exchange of newly kindled love. We both knew at that moment that our lives were back on track.

We lay naked on the beach, alone and undisturbed, until just before the sun rose. Then, hand in hand, like the lovers we once were and had now become again, we returned to the hut. There we slept in each other's arms until our desire woke us for more loving.

The week we spent in our island paradise was a rebirth for Hank, for me, and for our life together. We made love all day and all night, sharing our bliss with the sun and the moon and the sea and the sky. When we left to go home, we knew we would always be together.

Romance has stayed with us. We still feel it when we make love, even in the mundane surroundings of our bedroom. Sometimes, we make love by candlelight, and sometimes, we open the blinds to let moonlight flood our room. We play soft music on the stereo to bring back the memory of our romantic second honeymoon. That's what a real turn-on is.

FLOWERS

At forty-one, Arno is the owner of a large and successful chain of flower shops. In spite of his boyish build and sandy-colored hair, he gives the impression of stolidity. Meeting with us in one of the shops, his movements are slow and deliberate, his eyes constantly examining the stock. He is aware of every flower's indi-

vidual needs and patiently instructs his staff how to provide for them. At first, he
appears quiet and somewhat withdrawn, but when he talks about his flowers, his
excitement begins to show. His light brown eyes flash and his perfectly straight
white teeth gleam as he compares the fragrant blooms in his shop to the experi-
ences in his life.

A relationship with a woman is like a flower. It begins as a tiny bud and
then blooms into a magnificent object of beauty. The more you tend it,
the more beautiful it becomes. I am a successful florist because I know
how to care for my flowers. I'm a successful lover because I truly enjoy
catering to a woman. Especially when my relationship with her is at the
budding stage.

That's why romance turns me on. To me, the essence of romance is
taking the trouble to learn what my partner is all about—determining
her needs, her wants, her desires, and giving them to her without waiting for her to ask. You can't do that without listening, without being
finely tuned to her wavelength, without really caring. And I do care. I
really do.

Romancing a woman is almost certain to lead to the bedroom, but
that isn't why I do it. I get an incredible satisfaction, a sense of personal
worth, from pleasing her. Courtship is a challenge that absorbs all my
interest, almost to the point of obsession. For weeks on end, I think of
nothing but the woman I am courting. I might spend hours looking for
a certain small gift because I know it will have special meaning to her.
I'll hire someone to polish and wax her car while she's at work, or surprise her by having a fruit basket delivered right at lunch time. I devote
every possible ounce of effort to romancing her.

A woman can't help falling in love with a man who pays that much
attention to her, so a time usually comes when she offers commitment
and expects the same from me. For me, that's when the courtship and
the romance are over. The lovely bud has fulfilled its promise by spreading its petals and exhaling its perfume. But then the petals fall, and all
the potential is gone. There is no use tending a dying blossom and so I
move on to a new romance.

I had just ended a relationship when I first met Holly. I was melancholy about love's fading hues and thought I could drown my troubles by enrolling in a course at the local community college. The instructor was a well-known botanist and the course was Botanical Philosophy.

Holly was the most enthusiastic member of the class, perhaps because she was the only one not connected with the flower business. She was thirty-one and in the prime of her natural beauty. Her recent divorce had resulted in a settlement large enough to leave her without financial worries. Flowers were her hobby, and she spent most of her time working with orchids and exotic lilies.

One night after class, I invited Holly for coffee. Within minutes, she had revealed that she loved to take long drives through the countryside looking at wild flowers. The next day we took such a drive, and I listened for hours as she told me about her failed marriage. I may have been the first man ever to really listen to her. Her husband certainly hadn't. She said he had taken for granted everything about her.

As she spoke, I made mental notes of the things that turned her on, the little things that her ex-husband never gave her, perhaps because he didn't understand them. They were simple things, like walking on the beach and holding hands while watching the sunset. I learned about the foods she liked and the wines she enjoyed with them. She said she loved chocolates, but worried about her weight. I complimented her, saying I found her figure flawless, and meant absolutely every word. The next day, I sent her a huge heart-shaped candy box. Although the box was designed to hold three pounds of candy, I arranged for it to contain only three extremely rich chocolate truffles and an invitation to join me for dinner at home that evening.

I spent the afternoon getting the house ready for her visit. I filled it with fine specimens of the orchids and lilies she liked best. I designed the floral centerpiece myself, selecting blooms that would reach the perfect peak of their maturity just as we finished our dinner. The combination of fragrances made a heady perfume, turning the very air itself into an intoxicating drug.

I prepared the meal with care, cooking all the delicacies that she loved. Each course was accompanied by one of her favorite wines. When it was time for the next culinary treat, I removed the wine bottle from the table, even though we had not finished it, and replaced it with another of her favorites.

Soon after I won her stomach, I won her heart. With tears in her eyes, she told me over dessert that no man had ever taken such pains to please her. I asked how that could be possible. I said she was a goddess whom any man would be delighted to serve.

After dinner, we drove to a place that was well known in our town, a place where people came from miles around to watch the glorious sunsets. We got out of the car and stood in silence as the sky turned to flame. Just as the shimmering red ball dropped behind the horizon, I took her hand in mine and squeezed it gently.

Afterwards, we returned to my home for espresso and biscotti. When I served the coffee, I sprinkled a bit of chocolate powder on its surface. As she sipped and smiled her approval, I rose from my chair and bent to kiss her on the cheek. "I am honored to be with you," I whispered.

She turned her face to me and met my lips with her own. We kissed softly at first, my lips nibbling hers, her tongue dueling playfully with mine. She stood and held me in her embrace. I felt the softness of her feminine body pressed against me.

As if she were a feather, I lifted her and cradled her in my arms. She sighed and rested her head against my chest. "Make love to me," she whispered. Carefully, I carried her into the bedroom.

I laid her on the bed and stood over her, a look of admiration lighting my face. I touched one of the buttons on her blouse and hesitated. "May I undress you?" I whispered. I wanted her to know I would take nothing for granted.

Covering my hand with hers, she said, "Yes, undress me."

I fell to my knees beside the bed and laid my head on her bosom. "I am overwhelmed," I murmured. "Being with you makes me weak and strong all at the same time."

I undressed her slowly, stopping to admire her nakedness. She lay back languidly with her eyes closed, moving only to cooperate in the removal of her garments. I knew she was thinking about all the sexual disappointments she had experienced in her unsuccessful marriage, but I resolved to change that.

I listened to the silent messages her body sent. I did everything she had ever dreamed about, everything she had always wanted and never received. I knew where she wanted my lips even before she did. I knew exactly where to put my fingers, how to touch her, how to kiss her.

I filled my mouth with as much of her breast as it could hold, running my tongue over her palpitating nipple. I brought my fingertips lovingly across her belly, stroking reverently at the downy curls of her pubic triangle. I paused for her permission before placing my hand flat on her opening. She keened with desire as I explored her.

I made love to her for hours, keeping my clothes on out of respect for her sacred self. With my mouth and my hands, I kept her on the edge of climax. I strove for her total satisfaction, wanting only to extend it until her needs had been completely fulfilled.

Her face took on an angelic serenity when she realized that her pleasure was my only goal. Without speaking, she used subtle movements of her body to show me what parts of her ached for contact. I was receptive to her messages, bringing my lips to each of her cravings.

At last, she opened her eyes and looked lovingly into mine. Her hands reached for the front of my trousers, and I stripped swiftly, enjoying the hunger of her gaze. Lying beside her, I touched the warmth between her legs, silently begging her permission to enter.

"Yes," she murmured, rolling onto her side and putting one leg over my hips. "Come into me." She was so ready to receive me that I slipped easily inside her.

Our bodies began moving in graceful rhythm. I bathed in her soft warmth for a long time, exercising all my control to make her satisfaction certain. Finally, when her orgasm commenced, I let myself go. I was suffused with a feeling of potency and strength. I had pleased her as had no one before.

She stayed with me that night. The next morning over breakfast, I told her that she was the most beautiful and the most exciting partner I had ever been with. I described the feelings I had when she kissed me, when she told me to make love to her, when she opened herself to me. I said that being with her made me feel important. Every word was true.

Later that day, I had a messenger deliver three hybrid lily bulbs of a variety I knew she admired. I wrapped them in gold foil and attached a note thanking her for coming into my life. We saw each other again that night and many nights thereafter.

Whenever I discovered a new way to please Holly, I got turned on a little more. It seemed that the courtship would never end, but then, about a week ago, she said the magic words. We had gone to a little county fair and were exuberantly eating ice cream and Belgian waffles. Suddenly, she turned to me and with a serious look said, "I love you, Arno. I think I want to spend the rest of my life with you."

It was the apex. I had taken our romance as far as it could possibly go. Once a woman is sure that she is in love and starts talking about forever, she is bound to become oblivious to everything else. She will begin taking all my little efforts for granted, and romance will be dead. Tonight, when I see Holly, I'll have to find a way to say good-bye. Because romance is the only thing that turns me on. Without it, there is nothing.

When I was just a small boy, my parents said I always started things and never finished them. You might think that's true of the affairs I have with women. But my parents were wrong, and if you thought the same, you'd be wrong, too. All I set out to do is bring the bud to flower, and I always finish what I start.

2
I LOVE TO TEASE

"GIANT EGGPLANTS ATTACK CHICAGO! DETAILS AT ELEVEN."
Few people can resist a pitch like this one, and so millions will wait expectantly for the late-night news. Chances are, the story will turn out to be about a grocery truck that overturned on Lakeshore Drive, spilling its cargo of vegetables onto the Chicago thoroughfare. Once the viewers have tuned in, though, they're hooked. That the details don't live up to expectations doesn't really matter. Everybody knew there wasn't really an attack, and the headline brought fun to a mundane and otherwise unexciting traffic accident.

In the television business, that kind of announcement—one that makes a promise, which may or may not be fulfilled later that evening—is known as a "tease." It's a well-worn television trick, but it's one that never fails. It often works in other areas of life, too.

The tease is what makes circus-goers pay three dollars to look at a two-headed calf. Deep down, they know they are going to end up seeing some sort of fake. It's the promise, however, that brings them in. More correctly, it's the way the promise is presented. If it's really done right, customers don't even feel cheated. After all, circus-goers are out to have a good time, and the tease is part of the game.

Many people build that same sort of psychology into their sex lives.

To them, teasing is the salt and pepper lending exquisite flavoring to their eroticism. Some have elevated the use of this spice to a high art, promising sexual delights they have no intention of delivering in order to increase their partners' appetites.

Both stories in this chapter were told by tease artists. There is an important difference between them, however. For Annette, teasing is a way of life. She does it for her own amusement because she loves the game and the effect teasing has on her. For Seth, teasing is a profession, a means to a financial end. Although he enjoys it, he does it primarily to arouse others.

BLIND DATE

Annette, thirty-six, is a lawyer, but it's hard to imagine her wearing a conservative suit or carrying a briefcase into a courtroom. A mane of naturally red hair cascades over her shoulders and back, reaching almost to her waist. She is quite tall and slender, with full breasts that ride high on her chest and hips that are wide and sensuous. She wears skirts short enough to reveal the finely sculpted curves of her thighs and snug enough to highlight her firmly muscled buttocks. It is obvious that Annette likes to be looked at.

I love to tease men. That's what got me married. It's probably what got me divorced, too. That matrimonial experiment taught me a valuable lesson. I'm just not the kind of lady that ought to be married. I have too much fun being single. For me, life should be a never-ending string of sex-hungry men. My goal is to make them hungrier by exercising my teasing technique. Teasing is the thing that really turns me on.

It's funny. Just a few nights ago, I realized I even get a kick out of teasing myself. I was in the shower getting ready for a date—a blind date, I guess you'd call it. Colleen, my secretary, set it up. Colleen's roommate had gone out with him for a while, and now that they had broken up, Colleen thought Phil and I might hit it off.

She hadn't told me much about him, except that he was a lawyer specializing in divorce and that he had been divorced a couple of times himself. She also said that ever since he stopped seeing her roommate a few weeks ago, he had been letting everyone around him know how horny he was. My kind of guy.

I was thinking about him as I let the hot shower sting the skin of my breasts. Absently, I began soaping under my arms. Imagining his masculine hunger, I felt my nipples harden. My hands were drawn to them. I applied the soap gently and lovingly, making small circles around the tips of my breasts until I felt myself getting warm in the crotch.

I continued petting and soaping my nipples with one hand, while the other slid the soap slowly down my belly. I moved the creamy bar in a series of serpentine curves, coming closer to my wet curling hair. My heated vulva craved contact, and I almost accommodated it with my hand.

When I touched a corner of the soap to the swollen flesh of my clitoris, I felt my resistance weakening. Inside, my juices were churning. I desperately wanted to thrust a finger into the heated moisture and calm my body's begging desire, but for some reason, I did resist. I kept nudging the perimeter of my sex, lightly stroking hair and lips, but denying myself the satisfaction I wanted so much.

It would have been so easy to finish myself off with a few expert strokes as my clit was trembling with excitement and demanding release. But I think the enjoyment I got from teasing myself was more stimulating than an orgasm would have been. I kept it up, feeling my sex temperature rise and knowing all along that I was only a millimeter away from fulfillment. But I was careful not to cross the line.

I'm telling you about this to show you what an important role teasing plays in my sexuality. By the time I got out of the shower, I had worked myself up to a state of total sexual tension. I love to feel that way. While I was drying myself, I kept it at its peak. Whenever I felt the tension start to subside, I brought it back by pressing the towel against my mound or flicking my clit with the tip of a finger.

My arousal heightened as I thought about the evening that lay ahead. I slipped slowly into the black lace panties I had chosen for the occasion. The sides were cut high and narrow, barely covering my red bush, with maybe just a few rebellious strands escaping confinement. The black push-up bra I had selected was a match for the panties. I watched myself in the mirror as I snapped the clasp between my breasts. I liked what I saw.

I've got big breasts to begin with, and their size was amplified by the design of the bra. It supported and lifted to create a cleavage that excited even me. I could only imagine how my horny date would be affected when the minuscule dress I had picked out for the evening revealed the lacy lingerie.

My legs are tan enough and smooth enough that I can get away with not wearing hose. I like to watch a man's expression as he tries to decide whether my legs are really bare. I especially enjoy his surprise when he discovers that they are.

I glanced at my body, admiring myself while applying my makeup and fixing my hair. Noticing the time, I realized he'd be there any minute. Taking a black floor-length silk robe from the closet, I tossed it onto the bed. A few moments later, the doorbell rang. My timing was perfect.

When I went to answer, I left the robe where it was. Innocently, I concealed myself behind the door, opening it only as far as the chain bolt would allow. "You must be Phil," I said sweetly. "I'm sorry. I'm not quite finished getting dressed."

I knew, of course, that this was obvious to him because he could see me in the mirror on the wall. I could tell from the look on his face that he was enjoying the view. He was trying not to show it, but he just couldn't take his eyes from the reflection. I rotated my hips in a circle subtle enough to make him wonder whether it was an innocent movement or whether I was deliberately provoking him. Then I said, "I think I'd better go put on a robe," and shut the door abruptly.

I took my time before returning, knowing that he was anxiously waiting for another glimpse. I didn't let him have it immediately. Instead, I hugged the robe tightly around me as I led him into the living room and invited him to sit on the sofa. But while I was pouring him a drink,

I carelessly allowed the garment to fall open, giving him a good look at the front of my nearly naked body. When I caught him checking me out, I gasped in mock embarrassment, pulling the robe closed.

"Excuse me," I said, glancing away as if I were nervous about meeting his eyes. "I think I'd better finish dressing."

Walking into the bedroom, I went through the motions of closing the door, but made sure it remained slightly ajar. I positioned myself in front of the bedroom mirror, where I knew he could see me with a minimum of effort. Slowly I shed the silken wrap, turning in place under his surreptitious gaze. Then, with a quick motion, I picked up my dress and put it on over my head.

After a final self-appraisal in the mirror, I flung open the door in time to see him turning suddenly away. His flushed expression of excitement was tinged with childlike shame. He had been caught peeking. The night was just beginning, and I was already exerting my power over him.

I resolved to keep him in a state of constant arousal and confusion. As he assisted me into his low-slung sports car, I allowed my skirt to slide up so high that he could see the black lace crotch of my panties. I smiled when I caught his guilty glance. To keep him off balance, I tugged at my skirt in a feigned attempt to cover myself.

Inside the car he leaned across me to lock my door, and my breasts brushed lightly against his arm. I saw uncertainty flit across his face. Had the contact been deliberate, or was it an innocent accident? To increase his confusion, I pressed my back against the seat, as though trying to put space between my body and his arm. I knew the movement would emphasize the erectness of my nipples, straining against the thin fabric that barely covered them.

I was excited by my own antics. Probably, I would have been no matter what he looked like, but he was more attractive than I had expected—a pleasant bonus. He was tall, a good two inches taller than I. His hair was thick, and black, and obviously well cared for. His eyes were brown, like mine, with just a trace of cunning that befits a successful divorce attorney. I was looking forward to a stimulating bout of teasing, to last throughout the evening.

We went to a posh restaurant. While we dined, I found several excuses to touch him casually on his arm or shoulder. Once, I even placed my hand on his thigh for a brief moment, moving it away just as he began to realize what I had done. At about the same moment, his fingertips touched my leg. I could sense his rising interest as he encountered bare skin.

By the time we finished dinner, we were comfortable with each other and our conversation flowed smoothly. He suggested that we go dancing and have a few after-dinner drinks. That fit perfectly into my plan.

We wound up in a trendy nightclub, surrounded by other young professionals on the make. As we danced, I moved my body suggestively against his, noticing and enjoying the stiffness that was developing in his pants. The music was soft and seductive, perfect for slow dirty dancing. The couples around us were swaying provocatively, and we emulated their movements.

The slow dance provided an excuse to press myself against his erection. At first, I pretended I wasn't aware of it. Then, as if I had suddenly discovered his tumescence, I pulled back awkwardly, watching his smile of satisfaction fade to uncertainty.

I enjoy my ability to manipulate a man's emotions. The glorious sense of power it gives me is the most intense turn-on I know. I think I get a greater feeling of victory from winning a man over with my teasing than from winning a tough case in court. After a few drinks, Phil seemed to become a bit less cautious, so I decided to escalate my campaign.

On a trip to the powder room, I adjusted my bra and the neckline of my dress until I was sure that by leaning in a certain direction I would be showing Phil my erect pink nipples. When I returned to the table, I bent over to give him a preview. It worked. He immediately sprang from his chair to assist me into mine. He lingered over me to feast his eyes from above, making no attempt to hide his interest.

Phil wasn't showing signs of embarrassment anymore. Instead, he was looking directly into my cleavage, his trousers stirring in witness to his arousal. It was time for me to take control again. Twisting slightly in my chair, I grazed his bulge with my shoulder, letting him wonder whether it was an accident. Before he could be sure one way or the other, I moved away again and lifted my drink.

We sat for a while, sipping from our glasses and chatting. Occasionally, my leg brushed his under the table, but never long enough for him to know it was deliberate. My well-timed seductive smiles added to his confusion. Teasing another lawyer is the most fun of all. Male attorneys are usually so sure of themselves that I can't help getting a special feeling of satisfaction when I manage to rattle them with a touch or even a look.

When we got up to dance again, I melted into his arms, surrendering to his lead. I pressed the softness of my breasts against his muscular chest and moved my hands suggestively across his back. The rhythm was slow and sexy, and all the couples around us looked like they were screwing on their feet in time to the music. That kind of dancing was in at the moment, so when I put my arms around his neck and rubbed my body against his, he didn't know whether I was falling under his spell or whether it was just part of the dance.

I let one of my hands stray slowly downward until my palm was pressed into the small of his back. Almost imperceptibly, my fingertips continued their journey, nudging delicately at last at the place where his waist ended and his muscular ass began. I felt his pelvis rock forward, driving the swelling of his sex firmly against mine. My fingers pressed his buttocks, subtly encouraging his thrust.

Just as his breathing began to get raspy, the music ended. I stepped quickly backwards, leaving him with empty arms and an embarrassingly obvious hard-on. I glanced downwards and then, looking slightly away from him, said, "Oh, I think we'd better sit down." I was rewarded by seeing his face redden, like that of a teenager caught in a forbidden act.

I returned confidently to our table, feeling like a victorious matador who arrogantly turns his back to show power over the bull. In my head, the crowd was cheering, "Olé!" But the bullfight wasn't over yet. To keep it interesting, I had to restore some of his confidence, so as he pulled back my chair, I murmured, "You're a great dancer."

He smiled, his strength returning. "This place is getting warm," he said. "Maybe we ought to try somewhere else."

"How about my apartment," I suggested coyly. I just love to keep a man off balance.

At first, I thought he was going to stammer, but he composed himself almost at once. "That's a wonderful idea," he answered quickly. Acting before I could change my mind, he motioned to the cocktail waitress, and then, apparently not willing to lose time, he dropped some money on the table and assisted me out of my chair. Frustration shadowed his face for a brief moment when I excused myself to the powder room, but he recovered nicely, certain of eventual conquest.

I went directly to the phone in the ladies' room and dialed Colleen's number. She's been my friend for a long time, and I can always count on her. When she answered the phone, I just said, "Colleen, please call me at home in forty-five minutes. Exactly forty-five."

"OK," she said with a laugh. "I'm setting the kitchen timer right now." She knew I was up to something, even though she didn't know precisely what.

Turning to the mirror, I freshened my makeup and dabbed a few drops of perfume in strategic spots. There wasn't any rush. Phil would be impatiently, but obediently, awaiting my return.

Heading home in his Jaguar, I could see him watching me from the corner of his eye, hoping my neckline or hemline would slip. I kept myself covered without appearing to work at it. While stopped at a traffic light, he noticed an open liquor store. "Shall I go in and get us a bottle of champagne?" he asked suavely. The poor guy was so sure of his victory, I had to struggle to keep from laughing.

Pitching my voice low and husky, I said, "Sure, I think that's a wonderful idea."

By the time he came back to the car, I had rearranged my position and my clothing to create maximum excitement. The full curves of my breasts were exposed almost to the nipples, and my dress was so high on my thighs that another inch would have made it altogether superfluous. I heard his breathing become shallow. The confident attorney had turned into a little boy staring hungrily into the window of a toy shop.

Back at my apartment, I put ice in a silver bucket and placed two crystal flutes on a tray while he busied himself with the champagne bottle. He opened it like a man who had performed that task many times before. There was just the right volume of pop, and the cork ended up in his hand rather than bouncing off the ceiling.

I placed the tray on the low coffee table in front of the sofa, bending forward to give him another good look into the valley between my breasts. Then I went to the stereo cabinet and leaned over to study the CD titles and drop one into the player. I knew my skirt was riding up high enough in the back to show him the creases where my buttocks met my thighs and to let him glimpse the black lace of my panties.

After he poured the bubbling wine, I sat beside him, my hip pressed firmly against his. He handed me a glass of champagne and put his arm across the back of the couch in a confident and proprietary way. We leaned back and sipped slowly, our mutual excitement building in silence.

As his arm encircled my shoulders, his hand fell casually in front of me, his fingertips barely grazing the swell of my breast. My nipples hardened, desirous of his touch in spite of all my resolve. He moved slightly, his hand stroking me so softly that for a moment I wasn't even sure it was happening. It was a well-practiced maneuver, obviously drawn from his bag of seductive tricks. I liked it and permitted it to continue, allowing myself to forget for a second who was supposed to be teasing whom. Then I regained control, deliberately leaning forward to press the full curve of my breast into the palm of his waiting hand.

He was surprised and a little taken aback at having lost the initiative. For a moment, his hand remained motionless, not knowing quite what to do next. Maybe he was waiting for me to pull away again, as I had so many times that evening. When he realized that I wasn't going to, he began caressing my breast lightly, at the same time searching for my lips with his own. We kissed passionately, each of our tongues boldly invading the other's mouth.

His excitement was mounting and so was mine. When he slipped the straps of my dress down over my shoulders, I let him. And when he exposed the lace of my wispy black bra, I arched my back, offering him my breasts without shame. He was on them in a flash, his hot lips trailing wetly over my curves and lingering along the border where the lacy lingerie ended and the exposed smoothness of my skin began.

My fingers worked at the buttons of his shirt as his hands sought the clasp of my bra. He got it open, and my breasts sprang into his exploring grasp. The hardness of my nipples raked his palms with their heated arousal.

Reluctantly, he let me slip away as I forced the shirt off over his muscular arms. As soon as it was done, his hands returned to their exploration. He groaned when my fingers stroked his muscular chest, tangling in the coarse hair and playing over his tiny masculine nipples.

Suddenly, I stood. The music on the stereo was just right for my next move. I looked directly into his eyes, and with desire written all over my face, I swayed slowly and sinuously, removing my dress. Remaining were my filmy black panties and the unhooked bra, which I wriggled out of, my movement tearing a gasp from his throat.

Before he could take control of his own reactions, I rejoined him on the couch and fell once more into his embrace. I kissed him hard on the lips and began groping for the buckle of his belt. I had it open in an instant. I pulled him to his feet and finished the job, carefully unzipping his fly. A moment later, his trousers were tangled around his ankles and he was working his feet out of his shoes to step free of them.

He wore tight-fitting, pale blue, bikini-style shorts that showed him to be even better endowed than I had imagined. His briefs were loaded with the bulk of his genitals, the front jutting out before him to signal his desire. For a moment, I pictured myself letting go as the hugeness of him slid into me and dominated my being, but the image passed quickly. I like control too much to relinquish it.

Glancing unobtrusively at the clock, I hooked my thumbs into the waistband of his cotton underwear. The time was just about right. Gradually, I lowered the garment, exposing another inch of his hard flat abdomen. A few strands of his curling pubic hair came into view as I tugged the shorts lower. Then his briefs were down around his knees, and his erection was standing straight out from the jungle of hair at his crotch.

Just then the telephone began to ring. "Oh, fuck," he muttered. His glance implored me to ignore the interruption.

I let myself appear uncertain for an instant. Then, with feigned resignation in my voice and a triumphant giggle in my heart, I said, "I think I'd better answer it. It might be important."

I walked to the phone, knowing that his eyes were fixed on the flowing motion of my bottom under the lace of my skimpy panties. I picked up the receiver and turned to him, noticing that his erection was still with him, bobbing hopefully. It was difficult to keep myself from breaking up at the sight of him trembling with desire and hobbled by the underpants pulled halfway down his legs.

"Hello," I said into the mouthpiece. When Colleen identified herself, I said, "Oh, no, that's too bad." I glanced at Phil with an expression of frustration, adding, "Well, OK, then. I guess there's nothing else I can do. I'll be there as soon as I can." Colleen laughed and hung up.

When I returned to Phil, my face was expressionless. Without a word, I gathered my clothes from where they had been tossed to the floor and slipped back into my bra. "I'm so sorry," I said as I hooked it shut. "It's an emergency, and I'm afraid I'm going to have to leave."

I sidestepped his request for details by saying simply, "I'm sorry, it's a client. Privileged communications and confidential information. I don't think I ought to discuss it. And, anyway, there's no time. I've really got to run."

I rejected his offers of help and a ride, urging him to hurry into his clothes. Watching, I could feel the agony of his disappointment. That part really turned me on.

"When can I call you again?" he asked dejectedly, as I opened the door to let him out.

"Soon," I answered, my voice breathless with promise. "We've simply got to finish what we started."

His mood changed immediately, his face lighting up with renewed anticipation. "Great," he said. "I'll be in touch." He looked sure of himself again, almost cocky.

He just knows that he's going to score on our next date. But, of course, I have other plans. I'm not finished teasing him yet. For me, that's the biggest turn-on of all.

THE BIG TEASY

Seth, twenty-five, looks like he just stepped off the cover of a romance novel. Frequent sessions in a tanning booth give his skin the color of burnished bronze. His blond wavy hair is shoulder length. His piercing blue eyes seem to see deep into the core of people. At 6 2″, he is 195 pounds of finely sculpted muscle, the result of strenuous daily workouts.

I've got to keep myself in good shape. It's part of my profession, even though it's only a temporary profession. By day, I'm a graduate student in molecular biology, but at night, I take my clothes off for women. Sounds incongruous, I know, but some of my colleagues who hold down regular jobs as laboratory technicians have to work two or three weeks to make as much as I can make in a weekend, sometimes in a single night.

The pay is great and the tips are even better. I work through an agency that books me for bachelorette parties. I think the whole thing is a product of the women's equality movement. Lots of women feel that equality means they have to act just like men, so they find excuses for wild and raunchy parties and hire a male exotic dancer to entertain them, just the way men have traditionally hired strippers to jump out of giant cakes. Sometimes, it's a birthday party; sometimes, a commercial promotion. Lots of times, it's the night before somebody's wedding. People can always find a reason to throw a party.

I can get as much work as I want because I'm very good at what I do. I was born in New Orleans, the town they call "The Big Easy." So the people at the agency call me "The Big Teasy" because, let's face it, I dance, but I'm not really a dancer. What I am is a professional tease. The women eat it up, and they're willing to pay big for it. Besides, I won't deny that I love it, too.

Basically, my job is to twist and gyrate while the women sit around and scream. Sometimes, I think they're working at being as obnoxious as men. They stare at my muscles and leer at my crotch. They reach out to grab at me as I undulate around the room.

Most of the time, I stay just out of range, but part of being a good tease is deliberately misjudging the distance every once in a while and allowing some of them to succeed in touching me. It keeps the rest hopping on the edge of their seats with envy for the ones who copped a feel.

Of course, they don't just hire me to dance. I'm expected to take off my clothes. That's where the teasing is most important. I strip real slow. Sometimes, it takes half an hour before I get everything off.

There's never any question about how far I go. That's always negotiated and arranged in advance. It doesn't cost quite as much if I keep the G-string on. Even then I manage to pull it down far enough so that they'll all have a chance to get a little glimpse of the equipment. Just a peek. That's what makes them ask for me next time they call.

Most of the time they agree to go the extra hundred dollars to have me strip totally nude. When I do those shows, I spend a good fifteen or twenty minutes just removing the G-string. Naturally, I work them for tips the whole time. I move all around the room, posing and gyrating in front of each woman present. Sooner or later, one of them gets the idea of stuffing money into the G-string. I roll my hips for her, so that her fingertips graze my dick. Then they all want to do it, so I move around the room again.

You'd be surprised at how much money I take in that way. By the time I've made half a circuit, there are fives and tens sticking out of the waistband and thigh bands and more bills wadded up in the basket. The money is sweet, but so is the feeling.

What could be better than having a dozen or more women pay to touch me that way? It really turns me on to see how hungry they are for me, and to know that I am in total control. I'm the one who decides who gets to touch what and how far it's going to go. The idea is never to let them get all they want, because then they'd lose interest. Like I said, I'm real good at teasing.

That means I have to be strong. I can't control the situation unless I control myself. Don't think I'm not affected by all that touching and handling. I assure you, my cock wants to stand up and stretch, and it takes a lot of effort to keep it down, but I have to. Otherwise, the women who make it hard will be in control of me, instead of me being in control of them.

Also, my dance would look clumsy if my dick were sticking way out in front of me, so I manage to keep it in a state of semierection. That tantalizes the ladies even more. They can see it bulging, but the subconscious message is that it would take a very special woman to get this boy fully excited. That makes them all want to try. When they stuff money in my jock, they make a swipe at my balls or run their hand over my thighs and buns. I twist my body just out of reach, but I always make sure they get a little touch first. You'd be surprised at what an extra treat that is for them.

The way I see it, there's a subtle conflict at work here. They like watching me strip and show them my body. It excites them to grab at me. It gives them a sense of freedom. They all act as if they're snatching like crazy for my dick, but at that point, they don't really expect to succeed. They love getting a little-bitty feel, but most of them wouldn't really want a handful. Basically, they're all respectable women. Half of them are married and wouldn't think of cheating on their husbands and certainly not with all their friends watching.

A little rowdy fun is one thing, but actually taking hold of my cock would involve some social risks. Mostly, their efforts to touch me are just a game they're all playing. If I let them catch me, the fun would be over. They want me to tease them, so I just keep it up until, eventually, I do get the G-string off. That's when the show really begins. First of all, I've got a really big cock. Seeing it in all its glory will turn just about any woman on. Second of all, having a totally nude man in the room with them changes the atmosphere a little, puts the party on a different plane.

Once I'm completely naked, there are open looks of admiration. Even the inhibited ones feel free to stare. Some of the women who were only going through the motions a few minutes earlier forget their social fears and start getting real serious about getting their hands on me. If I was just in it for fun, I'd let them cop all the feels they wanted.

Hey, don't let this pretty face fool you. I'm straight, I assure you. I love to have a woman's hands on my cock, but I wouldn't make as much money as I do if I weren't "The Big Teasy." So I stay just far enough away to be a little out of reach.

Usually, the agency books me for a one-hour show. After getting totally naked, I have to dance around for another fifteen minutes or so. When the time's up, I make getting dressed part of the act. The women howl and groan as I pull my clothes back on, covering the sights they were enjoying so thoroughly. But sometimes, I don't exactly quit when the hour is up.

Technically, the agency doesn't know about this, and if word got out, it wouldn't do my future scientific career any good, but there are times when I make a private deal with the women throwing the party. What I mean is that they sometimes pay me to do more than dance and strip. This is where I can make some big bucks.

Usually, it's when they're out to give the guest of honor a special treat—a very personal and intimate gift, an erotic birthday present or something to help her kiss the single life good-bye. My job will be to give the lady an orgasm. Sometimes, they even tell me how they want me to do her. Maybe doggie-style, or orally. You'd be surprised at how specific they can be.

They always say it's going to be a complete surprise, but I know that when they get real specific, it's got to be because they told the guest of honor all about what was in store for her, and she told them what she wanted. Even when they don't tell me how to do it, it always ends up being pretty clear to me that the lady was expecting exactly what she got.

That's what happened just a few weeks ago. Three executive-type women, obviously well-off and very much used to being in charge, threw a party for their friend, Eva. She was about to get married—for the third time!

Her friends said Eva's first two marriages had ended because she was unfaithful to her husbands. She had vowed that this time would be different. She was going to walk the straight and narrow forever, so I was supposed to be her last farewell to promiscuity.

Money was obviously no object. In addition to what they were paying the agency, I was going to get five hundred for the night. As an added incentive, they said that afterwards they would ask Eva what she thought of me and give me a bonus, depending on how she rated my performance. Of course, I knew I had only their word for that, but I resolved to give it my best shot.

The night of the party, they sat Eva in a chair in the middle of the room, and I was to dance around her. The performance was supposed to be for her alone, but the other ladies would be there to see it. When they told me it was Eva's third marriage, the phrase "three-time loser" had popped into my head. When I saw her, though, I realized that she was anything but a loser.

She was exquisite. Her friends told me she was in her early forties, but she seemed a whole lot younger. She was tall and svelte, with emerald green eyes and smooth translucent skin over fine cheekbones. Her silky blond hair was soft and well cared for. Her tits were a little too high and a little too firm for any woman over nineteen. My professional opinion is that there was a team of plastic surgeons lurking somewhere in the background. Good ones, though, because she looked great.

I was wearing black lycra pants. They were tight and clingy, designed to really show off the basket and buns. For dramatic effect, I had on a ruffled white silk shirt with huge flowing sleeves that would whip through the air as I waved my arms.

The rest of the women sat in a circle around the room, hooting and hollering while I stripped for Eva. They screamed with delight when I let her undo my shirt buttons and unsnap the waistband of my pants. She opened my zipper very, very slowly. Apparently Eva was a bit of a tease herself.

When I was down to nothing but a G-string, I moved in close and pulled the elastic waistband away from my body to give her a good inside view of my semi-erection. The hungry look she gave me made it twitch uncontrollably. I decided to abandon my usual restraint and allow myself to harden. After that, I danced with my hard-on pressing against the front of the G-string.

The skimpy fabric was straining at its seams. I stepped right up in front of her, pumping my hips forward to bring my crotch closer and closer to her face. I raised one leg high in the air and swept it over her head, brushing lightly against her. She surprised me by planting a kiss right on my bulge, making the other girls shriek with laughter.

I hooked my thumbs into the waistband of the G-string and began to draw it slowly downward, but when about an inch of my hair was revealed, I pulled it up again, even higher than it had been before. It's one of my favorite tricks. The women screamed, "Take it off. Take it off," as I pulled the thong tight into the crack between my buns. When I turned to show Eva my ass, her friends all shouted even louder. I drew the G-string down again, letting the whole audience see my goldilocks. I could feel Eva's hand caressing the muscles of my butt.

With a practiced flip of my hips, I flashed my cock at the audience before pulling the G-string into place again and turning around. Now, facing Eva, I lowered it a fraction of an inch at a time, watching her eyes open wide as I finally dropped it to my ankles and kicked it across the room. When I heard the women roar, I knew that one of them had caught it.

Eva riveted her eyes to the tip of my erection, which was swaying sensuously in front of her face. I danced only for her as, by prearrangement, the other women slipped quietly out of the room. One by one, they moved past me, some of them patting my ass as they went by.

Within minutes, there were no sounds in the room but the music I was dancing to and Eva's husky breathing. We were alone. The hungry look in her eyes told me she wanted me. I took the initiative as I had been instructed to do. Reaching for her hands, I pulled her gently, but insistently, to her feet.

She followed my lead and began dancing in place to the funky beat of the sensuous music. As she swayed, I undressed her slowly and deliberately, opening one button at a time until her blouse was completely off. I stopped to admire the way her tits filled her pink cotton bra.

Using elaborate gestures, I passed my hands all around the softly swollen cups without actually touching them. There couldn't have been more than a dozen molecules of air between us. As part of my dance, I went through the motions of unhooking the bra's front three times, stopping just before it was actually undone. Finally, I managed to unsnap it without making any contact with her skin.

I removed it from her carefully, tossing it casually to the floor as her milky breasts came into view. Still scrupulously careful not to make physical contact, I moved the tips of my fingers in circles around her nipples. Holding my face close to those sweet soft bazambas, I exhaled slow heated breaths across their quivering pink tips.

I think this form of teasing made her even more excited than if I had actually been touching her. The nipples got harder, the long centers reaching out for me, the dark round disks crinkling up tight. I tasted the tip of each thick nipple with the pointed end of my tongue, so lightly that even I wasn't sure my tongue was really touching them.

Placing my hands on her hips, I gently pushed her back, increasing the distance between us. Then, with agonizing slowness, I tugged at the waist of her long tight-fitting skirt. I felt my cock aching with desire as I slowly lowered the skirt over her flared hips, until finally, I could see the soft pink material of her panties. I wanted to grab her pussy and hold it full in my hand, to fondle and caress it for my own pleasure and satisfaction, but purposefully, I continued the big tease.

After what seemed like forever, probably to both of us, the waist of her skirt was at the level of her midthighs. I let it go, and it slid elegantly to the floor. Gently directed by my touch, she stepped out of it and stood before me wearing nothing but the brief cotton panties. Her patch of hair made a plump cushion of the crotch. I could almost see the curling wisps of platinum through the cloth.

I fell slowly to my knees before her, bringing my face close to the covered mound without actually touching it. I inhaled deeply, savoring the scent of her heated sex. Then, through the thin material of her under-wear, I bathed her pussy with my hot breath. She sighed, and the next time I inhaled, her fragrance had become even more erotic.

I pressed my lips to the swollen triangle, placing a kiss there. Taking the damp material in my teeth, I began dragging it slowly down. By then, she was sobbing with excitement and moving her body to help me slip the panties off her, but in spite of her efforts, I made it teasingly slow. I didn't release my bite hold until the garment had reached the point where it would fall by itself. When it did, she continued standing there, her ankles connected by the sexy scrap of cloth.

When I placed my face near her pussy and inhaled again, I found my-self becoming intoxicated by her aroma. My teasing had brought her to a peak of arousal. I could tell by the sounds she was making and by the swollen redness of her tissues that she was desperate for me.

I breathed softly on her, heating her membranes still more with the warmth of my exhalation. Without knowing she was doing it, she arched her back to press her pussy against me. I continued caressing her with warm air, keeping the lips of my mouth just a fraction of an inch away from the lips of her vagina.

When at last I touched her hot sex, it was with nothing more than the tip of my tongue, which I flicked up and down and over her labia. Lightly, lightly, so lightly that the touch was dreamlike, leaving both of us uncertain that it was occurring. I could tell how much I was arous-ing her from the sounds she was making.

I lapped softly, moving my mouth over the entire opening between her labia and dabbing at her swollen clit, never using any more pres-sure than I had started with, never thrusting myself hard against her. Her moans were coming in a kind of primordial rhythm, and I knew from the spasmodic movements of her pelvis that she was getting close to an orgasm.

I concentrated on her clit, lightly jabbing at it with my tongue tip and stroking its length with the insides of my lips. The flavor of her excited pussy told me that she was approaching the peak. Then, suddenly, her fingers tangled in my hair, pulling my head tight against her. She was coming. I could feel it. I could taste it. I could hear it in her screams of passion.

When her spasms subsided, I eased her gently down to the carpeted floor. I positioned her on her back, spreading her legs with the light, but commanding, touch of my fingers. I began stroking and caressing her, reawakening her excitement before it completely quieted down.

I looked into her pussy as my hands played with the sensitive tissues around it. I watched as it flowered open again, hungry for more fulfill-ment. Delicately, I teased and fingered the swollen lips. Gently, I touched the sensitive nubbin that was beginning to peek out once more. This time I would give her all of me. I was going for the big bonus.

Kneeling between her thighs, I inched forward until the tip of my dick was almost touching her moist opening. With a slight movement of my hips, I brought it forward, so that only the very end of the rounded head nestled between her shining pink pussy lips. Hesitating, I whispered, "Do you want it?"

"Yes," her voice implored. "Give it to me."

Ever so slightly, I pushed forward until the entire head was buried snugly inside. Instead of thrusting forward and back, I rotated slowly, caressing her from within. I was so aroused by my own teasing that I had to exercise all my control to keep from blowing up inside her. I wanted her to come again, and I had to hold back until then.

I didn't have long to wait. Within minutes, she began to utter a se-ries of grunts, the second climax hitting her even harder than the first. I kept the tip of my cock almost motionless inside her the whole time, karezza fashion, until her orgasm was spent. Then, I pulled slightly back and let myself go, spurting my own juices onto her swollen tissues.

She lay there for a long time afterwards, her eyes tightly shut, her breath coming in long sobbing sighs. Eventually, I quietly rose and dressed to leave. She never opened her eyes, and she never said a word, but I know she must have liked my performance because her friends ended up sending me a huge bonus.

3

DIFFERENT STROKES

AS THIS BOOK DEMONSTRATES, PEOPLE BECOME SEXUALLY aroused in a great variety of ways. As a popular colloquialism puts it, "Different strokes for different folks." That phrase has special significance in study of erotic turn-ons because if anything comes close to being the universal arouser, it is touch, or tactile stimulation.

The sense of touch is probably connected with more forms of sexual arousal than any other. It is also the only kind of stimulation that can work independently of the mind. An unconscious man can be brought to erection by lightly touching his genitals. A sleeping woman can be brought to orgasm by gently caressing her clitoris.

Because genitalia are richly endowed with nerve endings, they are known as erogenous zones—areas especially sensitive to sexual stimulation by touch. Ancient Indian texts suggest that the armpits, throat, breasts, lips, and thighs are also erogenous zones. Modern writers add the earlobes, buttocks, anus, perineum, shoulders, upper back, abdomen, flanks, hips, fingertips, nape of the neck, and even the soles of the feet. If they leave anything out, it's probably because they just didn't think of it.

On a purely mechanical level, any touching of the body can result in a sense of pleasure. Just as a cat will begin purring when rhythmically stroked, a tense human is likely to relax when receiving a back-rub or massage. Prolonging the contact leads to sexual arousal in almost anyone.

For some people, however, stroking is the most potent of all possible turn-ons. It may be a form of foreplay that gives meaning to the intercourse that follows, or it may be an erotic end in itself. Many of the people who told us that stroking was what excited them the most found touching to be just as exciting as being touched.

The stories that follow show two different attitudes toward erotic stroking. For Esther, touch has nothing to do with her blindness, but it is an expression of the love that she feels is essential for a lasting relationship. On the other hand, Drew describes stroking sessions as "hands-only sex." He says that the excitement it brings him has nothing to do with who his partner is or how he feels about her.

TOUCH ME

Esther, thirty-one, is legally blind, but says she can perceive shape and movement. She walks with quiet assurance, handling her white cane almost as if it were a fashion accessory. She is 5'3" and describes herself as chubby, although we would call her voluptuous. Her curly brown hair is short, framing a round face, expressive in spite of the dark glasses that protect her eyes. Her voice is firm, but gentle. Esther teaches in a school for the blind.

Touch is very important to me. I began to realize that when I started losing my eyesight, at the age of eleven. My blindness was the result of a progressive disease, and my parents tried to prepare me for it by getting me instruction in braille while I was still able to see.

Braille is printed by a machine that makes a series of little raised dots on paper, each letter represented by a different combination of dots. At first, I thought my fingers would never learn to distinguish one combination from another, but eventually, I found out how very discerning the sense of touch can be.

I am aware of the stereotype that all blind people use their fingers for eyes, but that's not necessarily true. Alex, my ex-husband, had even less sight than I, but never appreciated the pleasures of touch. I sometimes help out at a hospital by counseling people who are losing their vision, and I was called in to talk to Alex. Poor Alex. He lost his sight all at once, in an auto accident.

I ended up spending a lot of time with him, and we fell sort of in love and got married.

I tried to teach him braille, but he was never willing to develop the necessary sensitivity. He said he would just have to do his reading by listening to tapes. He was very angry about his blindness and seemed to carry that anger into everything he did. It was even evident in the way he made love to me.

Although "made love" isn't the right expression. It was too quick and brutal to be called lovemaking. It seemed so impersonal. He never petted or stroked me; he grabbed me. I almost felt like I was being mauled. Then he would mount me, enter me, thrust a few times, and it was over. There was no softness, no comfort, no tactile communication. I always felt loss, rather than gratification, after sex between us.

I tried to talk to him about it, but it never got me anywhere. Maybe I didn't use the right words. I said I wanted to know his body completely and he to know mine, by taking more time to touch and feel. He wouldn't even listen.

I guess there were other problems with our marriage, but to me, that was the main one. Anyway, nothing really worked out for us. After less than three years, we decided to call it quits. We were living in a nice condo development, with lots of features that made it easy for me to get around, and I wanted to stay there. Alex said that was all right with him because he wanted to leave the state. So he moved out, and we let the lawyers end our relationship.

I answered their questions and signed papers when they told me to. Most of the time, I was all right with it. When thoughts about my life started to get me down, I would tell my troubles to my neighbor Rafael.

Rafael had moved into the building about two years earlier, soon after his wife died. He said he just couldn't stand living in what had been their house, so he sold it and bought the condo. He was a good friend to me and to Alex, helping us on those occasions when we absolutely needed the use of a pair of eyes.

After Alex moved away, Rafael and I would have coffee together a couple of times a week. When I was feeling low, he had a way of joking me out of it. Most of the time, I felt fine, though.

Then one day, the lawyers called to say the divorce was final. I didn't think it would affect me at all. It was nothing but a formality at that point. But when I hung up the phone, I was terribly depressed. Since then, I've heard that mine was a pretty common reaction, but at the time, it was almost overwhelming. I just felt like I wanted to start crying and never stop. I had never felt that way before, and it frightened me.

I sat alone until nightfall and then realized I had a desperate need for company. The next thing I knew, I was standing in front of Rafael's door, pounding on the wood with my knuckles. It opened, and I felt Rafael's presence. All at once, a rush of tears began and I wept hysterically.

For a moment, I stood alone and vulnerable, racked by sobs. Then, Rafael put his arms around me and brought me into his apartment. He didn't even ask what was wrong. He just held me, letting his strength flow into me.

He was patient with me as he held me close to his chest. His powerful arms gave me the security and comfort that I sorely needed. His voice was soft and soothing. One of his hands gently kneaded the tension from my upper back while he tenderly caressed my hair with the other. My sobs began to subside as his touch quieted and calmed my trembling body.

I wrapped my arms around his muscular shoulders and cuddled up close against him. I felt safe and strangely content with my body pressed to his. The isolation that had so depressed me was gone. I was not alone. The physical contact between us was a shelter against loneliness and pain.

But then I began feeling something else. I tried stroking his hair the way he was stroking mine, but found myself wanting to tangle my fingers in it. His face brushed against my forehead, and instantly, I craved to feel his mouth with my own. I tilted my head back, and suddenly, we were kissing.

It started as a hesitant unspoken question that each of us answered with the pressure of our lips. The kisses were warm and soft, almost loving. As we kissed, his fingers explored me, traveling slowly across my back, tracing the lines of my neck and ear. He held my face in his hands. The effect was hypnotic, tranquilizing.

I touched him, too, sculpting the swell of his muscles with my fingertips, my hands roaming over his chest. I slipped my fingers between the buttons of his shirt, lightly grazing his bare skin. I had never touched Alex that way. It was thrilling.

I no longer felt consumed by anxiety. I was still trembling, but with a strange new erotic need. I guess I had never in my life experienced sexual satisfaction, and all the years of frustration had suddenly come to the surface. I wanted to touch Rafael all over and to feel him touching me.

I slowly unbuttoned his shirt, feeling the warmth of his skin as I uncovered it. I felt his breathing slow and deepen, as if he were struggling to control it. When his shirt was open completely, I caressed his chest, my fingers lightly touching his erect masculine nipples.

I was acutely conscious of his hands, working carefully to unzip the back of my dress. There was an urgency to his movements, but he did not hurry. Instead, he savored every bit of contact with my body, even with my clothing. He massaged the bare skin of my back, running his hands lightly over the straps of my bra. I could feel goosebumps running up and down my body.

We seemed to stand there forever, undressing each other bit by bit and feasting tactilely on each other's flesh. I loved the feel of his fingertips as they discovered the unique personality of my skin. He read me with his hands, committing me to memory, and offered his body for me to do the same.

We learned things about each other that I had never shared with

Alex. Our physical exploration was a foreplay that began before we touched each other's sexual parts. When we were completely nude, we found our way to Rafael's bed without breaking contact. Carefully, he lifted me and laid me on the mattress, immediately enveloping me in his arms and pressing himself full-length against me.

We touched each other for hours, not just with our hands, but with all the parts of our bodies. I still remember the feel of his thigh against my breast, of my ear against the small of his back. I inspected the texture of his elbow with the tip of my nose. He pressed the sole of his foot against the swell of my soft round belly.

He lay on his back while I rubbed my cheek over his entire body. When I came to his groin, I inhaled his manly fragrance. I buried my face in the dense fur at the base of his belly and nuzzled the crease where his leg joined his torso. I sensed the presence of his erection right there next to my face. I brushed my lips against it, thrilling to the silky smoothness. Then I nibbled my way down his leg, kissing each of his toes before moving to the other leg and working my way back up again.

All the while, he was touching me everywhere, petting my shoulders and breasts, caressing my buttocks, placing his palm flat against my heated crotch. His movements were patient and unhurried, with no goal but the experience itself. Somewhere, in the secret depths of my instinctual unconscious, I had always known it should be like this.

We rubbed our bodies together, like two orchestral instruments complementing each other in sensual harmony. We spooned, the entire front of his naked body pressed against the entire naked back of mine. We fit so well, and it felt so wonderful. We needed no words to express our thoughts, and none of our wants or desires went unfulfilled.

At last his erection reached out for me, and I opened to receive him. He entered me slowly and tenderly. His penetration was the ultimate caress, deep inside me. My climax began immediately, the first I had ever shared with another person. It was unlike anything I had ever known or imagined. Throughout its paroxysms, I felt secure, certain that Rafael would not leave me until I was truly and completely satisfied.

The orgasm seemed to last forever, and when it ended, another began. I thought I would pass out from the intensity of the pleasure. At some point, I was aware that he, too, was reaching completion. When I felt him flooding me, I experienced a sense of peace and serenity.

Our bodies remained intertwined for a long time afterwards as we lay in silence, still drawing solace from the contact. I stayed with Rafael that night, and towards morning, we made love again. It was every bit as comforting and satisfying as the first time.

I'd like to say that Rafael and I fell in love, got married, and lived happily ever after. But I guess that wasn't really what that night was about. We never even went to bed together again after that. We're very good friends, but we're not in love.

What I learned from my experience is that when love comes along, touching is a way of expressing it. And my soulmate—where ever he is—will have to feel that way, too.

HANDS ONLY

Drew is thirty-five and drives for a parcel company. His hazel eyes almost match the color of his company uniform. His head is covered with thick curls of brown hair, but his bushy mustache is white. He loads his truck every morning and carries heavy boxes all day long. He is big all over, standing six feet tall and weighing 240 pounds. He is built like a tower of strength, but his hands are graceful—almost elegant.

To me, nothing is as exciting as a nice thorough hand job. I love giving them, and I love getting them. I don't know why, but hands-only sex is a fantastic turn-on.

It's awfully hard getting a woman to understand that, though. With my wife, it's impossible. Lord knows I've tried. When I'd ask her to jerk me off, she'd start out willing enough. She'd begin by stroking and rubbing me, but somehow she never finished that way. She'd always end up going down on me for a while and then climbing on top and putting me inside her. That's good, too, and I was usually so turned on by then that I just gave in and let go, but when it was over, I always felt a little let down and even a little bit resentful.

I think the trouble is that, to my wife, intercourse is always the goal. She believes it's the only legitimate way to get sexual satisfaction. Everything else is just foreplay. In her heart, she thinks there's something perverted about having orgasms any other way. On the occasions when I did assert myself and insist that she finish me with her hands, her heart wasn't in it. I might as well have been masturbating myself.

The same thing happens when I try doing her manually. I can't make her see the hand job as an end in itself. She thinks the only reason for me to finger her is to turn her on. Once she gets all wet and tingly, she wants something more, wants to move on to what she calls "the real thing."

She even pulls my hand away sometimes, yanking my finger right out from inside her. She grabs me by the hair and pulls my head down onto her. One way or another, she eventually insists that we have intercourse. I know I could get her off by hand if she'd only let me finish. And I know she could have a wonderful orgasm that way, but I just can't make her comprehend.

Actually, I've only known one woman who really understood the pleasures of hands-only sex—Adrienne. We went out together a few times before I met my wife, but we never had anything to talk about. We didn't like the same kinds of movies. We didn't like the same kinds of activities. I don't even think we particularly liked each other. The only thing we had in common was that we both loved hand jobs.

After a date, we'd go back to her place and sit on the couch fooling around. We never went in the bedroom. We never even kissed. I'd just get my hand into her pants and play with her. She liked my hand so much that she would just sit back and let me do whatever I wanted, for as long as I wanted. She always came that way, but not until I had been doing her for a good long time.

Sometimes, she'd take everything off from the waist down so I could have easier access, but it was also exciting to do her with all her clothes on. I might even keep my hands outside her panties the whole time, rubbing her through the wet cloth.

She wasn't interested in having her breasts touched or being caressed elsewhere. She wasn't interested in having me go down on her. And she certainly wasn't interested in intercourse. She just liked to be masturbated.

After she came, she would do me the same way. I just lay back on the couch with my eyes closed and turned myself completely over to her. She would open my pants and reach inside to bring out my pecker, or she would pull my pants and shorts halfway down my thighs and expose my whole crotch. Once in a while, she would remove my clothes entirely, so I could spread my legs and so she could really get her hands in there.

She never touched me with her mouth. She never kissed me with her lips. She never pressed her hot body against mine, like they do in books and songs. I don't think the two of us were ever undressed at the same time, and neither of us was ever totally naked. She just jerked me off. She was an expert at it because she genuinely loved the process.

As good as she was, though, it wasn't enough to sustain a relationship. After a while, Adrienne and I just stopped seeing each other. Soon after that, I met my wife and fell in love. She and I had plenty to talk about. We enjoyed going to ball games together, and we liked watching the same TV programs. We were good companions.

It still feels great to wake up next to her and to see her smiling at me across the breakfast table. I love lying in her arms at night and feeling her kiss my face as I'm falling asleep. I love her. I truly love her. Most of the time, our sex is very good, but without those hand jobs, life can get awfully frustrating.

Then about three years ago, a funny thing happened. Stuff like this makes me feel that life is like a movie—like some writer or director has it all planned out right from the opening scene. One morning, when I went in to pick up my truck, the dispatcher said, "Hey, Drew, come over here and meet the new guy."

The new "guy" turned out to be a woman—Adrienne. I couldn't believe my eyes. I hadn't seen her in twelve years. In fact, I had heard that she moved to the other end of the country, yet here she was working in the same place as me.

After work that day, we met in the garage again and started to shoot the breeze. She suggested we have a Coke together, so we walked across the street to the little coffee shop where all the drivers hang out.

She started telling me about the things that had happened to her in the last twelve years, but I wasn't paying much attention. I had never really been interested in her, and I still wasn't. As she spoke, I found my mind wandering back to those evenings we spent on her living room couch masturbating each other. I was getting hard, right there under the table.

Trying to get my mind out of my crotch, I talked about my wife and kids. How they were doing in school and that sort of stuff. Adrienne didn't look all that interested either.

She said she had taken a shot at marriage, but it didn't work out. For the past few years, she had been living with another woman, who she referred to as her significant other. They sort of loved each other, but they weren't lesbians. They once tried sex together, thinking they might be, but that didn't work out either.

Then it happened. The thing that changed my life. She said, "You know, the only decent sex I ever had was when you and I got each other off with our hands. I wish I could find somebody to do that with now. Life would be pretty good if I could get some of that."

Her comment made me think. My life was already pretty good, but there was something missing, something I craved so much that I found myself resenting my wife for not fulfilling the need. Maybe Adrienne and I could help each other out.

"I'd give it to you," I said. "If you'd give it to me."

"But you're married," she objected. "I wouldn't want to break up your happy home. Anyway, I don't want a love affair. It's too complicated. It's always been obvious you and I aren't meant for each other. We never had anything in common, except that one thing."

"That's what I mean," I said. "I'm not talking about a love affair either. I'm just talking about that one thing. We don't have to go out on dates or go through the motions of having any kind of relationship at all. We could just get together once in a while and give each other a hand job."

I could see that the idea rang a bell somewhere inside her. She got a dreamy look in her eyes, and I knew she was remembering the sexual satisfaction we had been able to give each other in the old days. "How about tomorrow," she said. "I'll meet you somewhere and we can do it right in the back of the truck." I felt my pulse quicken. "I'll bring a blanket," she added.

The following day, we met during our lunch break, meaning we had exactly one hour to do the deed. We parked about a block apart in a heavy-traffic business district, climbed into the back of her truck, and closed the door behind us. There was something really exciting about the idea that life was going on all around us outside the truck, but that inside was a private little world of hands-only sex, where no one could see us.

As soon as the door closed, she unbuckled her belt and pulled off the brown trousers of her uniform. She wasn't wearing any underwear, and I became intensely aroused by the familiar sight of that dark tangle of hair. I watched her bend to spread a blanket on the truck's floor, admiring the view from behind. Then, with no preliminary, she lay down on her back and spread her legs.

I sat on the blanket beside her and went straight for the goodies. Just like the old days—no foreplay, no breast play, just pure masturbation. I started stroking her lightly, watching her open until her pussy was grinning at me. She was shining with moisture already, and I had just gotten started. She was totally submissive, letting me do anything I wanted, trusting me to please her without needing direction. She knew how much I loved doing it and so she knew I would do it well.

I played with her for a good thirty minutes, bringing her to the point of orgasm at least ten times. When I sensed that she wanted release, I kept up the stimulation, without any break. "You can come now," I whispered, as I felt her going over the top.

Her body thrashed a lot when she came. I think it was because she was trying to be quiet and had to do something to let out the nuclear energy that had been building up for so many years. I know it was the best orgasm she'd had in a long time.

After she had a moment to catch her breath, I started taking my pants off. As I dropped my shorts and stepped out of them, she put her clothes back on. It was my turn on the blanket.

I lay on my back, my hard-on sticking up like a flagpole. I hadn't been this excited in so long that I was afraid I would come before she even touched me. But when her fingers encircled me, all my worries went away. I remembered how good she was at giving me hand, and I just surrendered totally.

I don't know how long it had been since she jerked a man off, but she certainly hadn't lost any of her skill. It was a masterpiece of a hand job. When she was done, I felt like a totally new person.

In bed that night, I thought about my terrific lunch hour with Adrienne. It made me hot, so I turned over and began kissing my wife. I did all the things she liked, finishing off with intercourse that went on until she was totally satisfied. I was satisfied, too, and afterwards, I didn't feel the slightest sense of letdown or resentment.

Adrienne and I still get together for lunch every now and then, whenever one of us feels we really need it. We park in a different part of town every time and take turns doing it in her truck or mine. We also take turns about who goes first.

My home life is better as a result. I'm enjoying sex with my wife more than I ever did before. She is, too. I don't even feel like I'm cheating on her. It isn't Adrienne that turns me on. It's just the things we do to each other with our hands.

4

SEX TALK

FOR CENTURIES, OUR SPECIES HAS CLUNG TO THE MYTH that human beings are the only creatures that can communicate by the use of language. Most of us embrace it still, even though the myth has been shattered. Whales have a vocabulary of sounds with fixed meanings. The same is true of apes and birds. Bees tell each other where the nectar is with the movements of their bodies. Somebody even taught a gorilla to converse with humans in American Sign Language.

Although the use of language isn't unique to Homo sapiens, we probably use it more effectively than other animals. All creatures can communicate with each other about sex, but humans talk about it more than any other life form. We talk about it before having sex. We talk about it after having sex. Some of us talk about it while having sex.

To some extent, most of the people we interviewed found it exciting to discuss sexual matters. Several gave that as their reason for responding to our request for information. One man said that filling out our questionnaire about his sexual activities aroused him so much that he masturbated several times while writing answers to the questions. Some couples discuss their sexual memories as a way of reexperiencing the activities they most enjoyed. Others use sex talk on dates as a way of finding and stimulating potential partners.

Perhaps the stories in this chapter will shatter another myth—the one that says talkers aren't doers, and people who talk about sex don't usually get much of it. We chose stories told to us by people who not only like talking about sex, but who say it's the activity that turns them on the most. Ray and his wife have used sex talk as an adjunct to their open marriage. When they discuss the details of their extramarital affairs with each other, they feel they are making those affairs part of their relationship. Liz uses sex talk to relive the intensely sexual relationship she had with two other women before she married. Telling her husband about the sex acts she and her friends performed allows her to share the experiences with him as well.

THE BAR GAME

At forty-five, Ray is tall and broad, with wide shoulders and thick arms. His bulging muscles ripple with every move he makes. A dark tuft of thick brown hair shows through the open collar of his shirt. Ray's expression becomes serious as he explains why he needs every muscle he's got. For the past eighteen years, he has worked as a physical therapist.

My wife, Surya, and I are both very body-oriented, but talk is the thing that turns us on the most. Sex talk, that is. It was that way between us right from the start.

I met Surya in the very first physical therapy office I worked in. I had just gotten my license, and she was on the way to getting hers. We were attracted to each other right away, even though both of us were involved with other people.

One night I asked her to join me for a drink after work, and about an hour and a half later, we were rolling in bed together. The sex was fantastic, maybe because we were both so body-oriented. Anyway, we saw each other again and again.

I knew that Surya spent three or four nights a week with her boyfriend, and she knew that I was sleeping with several other women, but the situation didn't bother either of us. As a matter of fact, we discovered by accident that it was a turn-on. Once, when we were in bed, she casually said something about her boyfriend, and I asked her to tell me how the two of them made love. When she started describing their coupling, I found myself getting very aroused. I wanted to screw right away, but she insisted that I first describe sex with one of my girlfriends. I could see that she got aroused by it, too.

After that, we'd play the sex-talk game every time we got together. Then a funny thing happened. One day, Surya told me that her boyfriend had found out about us and had broken off with her. The day before that, by coincidence—or maybe it wasn't coincidence—the woman I had been seeing threw a tantrum because she learned she wasn't the only one in my life, or in my bed, anyway.

Surya and I both found our partners' behavior puzzling. Why should her boyfriend care if she had some fun with me or any other guy? Why should my lady friend complain about what I did with others, as long as there was enough left for her? After all, Surya's other sex partners were no problem for me, or mine for her. In fact, we got off on telling each other about them.

I guess that was the night our relationship started getting serious, the night we fell in love. We both liked the idea of being free spirits, of loving without being possessive. We understood, right from the start, that it would be OK for each of us to have sex with others. We agreed to have an honest open relationship. About a year later, it became an honest open marriage.

Any time my new wife would tell me not to expect her home that night, I would know she had a date with a guy and would probably end up in bed with him. And whenever I felt like sleeping with another woman, it was just as easy for me to tell her. The best part was the hot times we'd have with each other later on, talking about the things we did with others.

At first, we regarded sex with others as an activity that took place outside our marriage. Eventually, we realized that it wasn't outside our marriage at all. For both of us, the most satisfying sex of all was the sex we had with each other while talking about our little affairs. It seemed like the real purpose of being with others was to give us something to tell each other about.

We took sex talk to the ultimate extent when we started playing what we called "The Bar Game." That, too, was something we discovered quite by accident. We had gone out together for a drink to a place we didn't know. Once inside, we recognized that it was a singles bar, one of those pickup places. We had each been in plenty of them before, but never in this one.

I was standing at the bar, waiting for Surya to get back from the ladies' room, when a blond woman started flirting with me. First, she made sure to press her breasts against me as she squeezed in beside me in the crowd. Then, she asked if I'd like to buy her a drink. She started that heavy breathing stuff that goes along with the pickup game, and I found myself getting kind of turned on. She wasn't particularly good-looking, but she had a decent body. She was telling me in every possible way that she was available, but I didn't plan to do anything about it since Surya was my date for the evening.

Then, out of the corner of my eye, I saw Surya standing a little distance off, watching and smiling. Her expression was telling me to go ahead, to take it as far as I wanted. So I leaned over and whispered some trash in the blonde's ear—something about how good she looked in her low-cut dress. While I was whispering, I nibbled a bit. I could tell that she was ready.

Casually, Surya moved up to the bar on the other side of the blonde, as if she didn't know me. She pretended not to be paying any attention to us, but I could see her watching in the mirror. Keeping an eye on her, I said to the blonde, "Maybe we ought to go someplace else."

Breathlessly, she responded, "My apartment's only a couple of blocks from here." She was obviously hot to trot. I could see Surya nod slightly, letting me know that it was all right with her.

The blonde and I left and went straight to her place. Once inside, she wasted no time, stopping only long enough to unzip the back of her dress before throwing her arms around me and pressing her lips to mine in a deep and passionate tongue kiss. We peeled each other's clothes off as we groped each other's bodies. Within minutes, we were down and dirty on the carpet, screwing like mad.

After a quick one, we went into her bedroom and did things more slowly. I went down on her for a while, and then she went down on me. We screwed again, this time patiently and thoroughly.

When I left there, about two hours after I arrived, I was tired and spent, but flushed with the special excitement that comes from having a new partner for the first time. I was looking forward to telling Surya all about it.

When I got home, I was disappointed to find that Surya wasn't there. I figured maybe she had picked someone up, too. When she came in a little while later, the look on her face confirmed it.

As I took her in my arms, I could smell the scent of fresh sex all over her. Suddenly, I was ready for more. I lifted her up and carried her into the bedroom, depositing her on the bed and pushing her skirt up all the way to her hips. Her panties were pulled tight into her crack. As I placed my face between her thighs, I slipped a finger into the crotch and pulled it to one side. The material was soaking wet and so was her vagina.

I started kissing the outside of it, inhaling deeply to savor the musk of her sex. I licked her and nibbled at her, making her clitoris hard. "I've been fucking," I heard her say. Her words went straight to my gonads.

"Tell me about it," I murmured, returning to the softness of her vulva.

She began describing the guy who started talking to her a few minutes after I left the bar. They had gone to a hotel, where he asked her to stand in the middle of the bed while he slowly undressed her, licking and caressing each part of her body as he exposed it. She told me that she had stood with her legs far apart as he crawled under her and ate her from below. I could tell by the way her clitoris jumped and twitched that telling me about it was turning her on.

It was doing the same to me. I performed cunnilingus on her while she told me how his mouth had been right where mine was at that moment. When she talked about the way his tongue flicked over her vulva, I tried to do the things he had done as she so vividly described them. It excited me tremendously to suck on her clit only a few hours after another man. I loved hearing her tell me, in detail, about where he had placed his lips or how he had used his teeth. The thing was, I knew that she thought I was better than him. Otherwise, she wouldn't be home with me.

While she spoke and while I made love to her, I worked us both out of our clothes. Then I started moving my mouth higher, across her fragrant delta of Venus and over the smooth skin of her firm belly. Her breasts loomed above me. At this moment, they were mine, and this moment was all that mattered. I trailed my tongue tip between them, climbing higher and higher until I was sucking gently on her nipples. Then I kissed her warm and tender mouth.

We lay in each other's arms, our nakedness melding, our passion flowing through and between our bodies to connect us as one. "What did you do to her?" Surya asked in a husky whisper, as my fingers stroked the globes of her buttocks. "How did you fuck her?"

"We did it on the floor," I answered. "The first time, anyway." My hand was stroking her vulva now, feeling her wetness seep over the labia as she gushed with excitement.

Surya's voice was high, her throat tense with excitement. "How many times did you fuck her?" she asked. "Was she good?"

"She was very good," I answered, slipping one finger into Surya's vagina and feeling it close around me. "She was tight. Like you." I rammed hard, driving my finger in search of her G-spot.

I felt my wife's hand stroking down my body and across my belly to reach for my erection. As she began petting it lightly, I thought of her doing the same to the other man she had been with that night. I was conscious of my penis jerking and pulsing with life as the memory of her words made my head whirl with excitement.

"When I first got inside her, her muscles started to ripple," I said. "I think it had been a while since she got any because she was hotter than the hinges of hell."

I could tell by the reaction of Surya's body to my fingering and sex talk that she was hanging on every detail. Each word turned her on a little more, elevating her body heat. "I really got lucky tonight," I said. "First the wildcat and now you."

"She was the lucky one," Surya murmured, her vulva snapping at my driving fingers. She jerked roughly on my organ. She always knows exactly what I want and exactly how I want it—when sex should be soft and gentle and when to make it hard and rough.

"Did she suck on your penis?" Surya whispered. "I sucked on his." Her fingers made a tight circle around my erection, pulling it up and down. I could feel my joyjuice oozing as I pictured her fellating another man. The vision drove me wild with desire.

Sensing my excitement, she said, "He was thick and big, and my mouth was filled with him." She manipulated my penis with both hands, stroking and pulling and twisting lightly. "He whimpered and cooed and aaahhed when I rolled my tongue over him," she whispered, "and he got louder when I started playing with his scrotum. He tasted like salty candy."

As she spoke, I felt her fingertips roaming over my bloated sac, gently rolling my testes while her other hand pumped my phallus up and down. "Did he come?" I asked her. I was breathless with excitement at the thought of her giving an orgasm to another man.

"Yes," she whispered, "but not right away." Her hips bucked as I penetrated her repeatedly with my fingers. She was so excited that she was having trouble getting the words out. "I kept bringing him to the edge and then backing away, just like I'm doing to you."

I had been trembling on the brink of orgasm, and she knew it, drawing back just in time. She was an expert at reading my signals. I imagined her reading his the same way. The waves of climax were rising in me, but she kept them from breaking out of their self-imposed confinement.

Two of my fingers stroked and massaged her inner vaginal walls, while my thumb made lazy circles around the swollen button of her clitoris. It had drawn back inside the protection of the delicate pink dome that surrounded it. I knew that was a sign of her impending orgasm.

Her excitement made her reckless, letting me bring her closer and closer to the point of no return.

She spoke hesitatingly, struggling to control her vocal cords as her imminent climax demanded all her attention. "When . . . he . . . came . . . ," she stammered, "I . . . swallowed . . . his . . ." Then the words stopped, and her mouth fell open, letting out a strangled gasp. Her eyes were closed tightly, and I knew from her twisted grin that the orgasm was upon her.

I pictured his organ in her mouth. I pictured us. I pictured them. I pictured the blonde. I pictured my lovely wife's lovely vagina. And I started to come.

I felt the hot shots flying from my pulsing penis to splash onto my chest and belly. I was suffused by a feeling of total freedom as I spurted. I was fully immersed in visions of my wife's pleasure with another man and my pleasure with another woman.

Our sex talk had carried us to heights most people only hope for. No matter how many other partners each of us might have had, there was never anything as stimulating as the sparks our erotic conversations ignited. We went on making love until exhaustion overcame us. Then we drifted off to sleep, completely fulfilled and nestled securely in each other's loving embrace.

We continued to play the bar game. A few times we even made a contest out of it, trying to see which one of us would succeed first in picking up a temporary partner. It was fun, but the best part was always the time we spent together afterwards, exchanging stories and making love.

Of course, we don't do that sort of thing anymore. Nowadays, casual sex with strangers is liable to kill you. AIDS is a very scary disease. Surya and I have both been tested repeatedly, and thank goodness, we somehow managed to escape infection. Now we have a strict understanding. No sex for either of us with anybody else.

The funny thing is we don't really miss it. Sex talk is still the most exciting part of our lovemaking. Even though there are no new escapades to talk about, we've still got plenty of stories to share from the days of our open marriage.

If you really use this story in your book, there's something I'd like to say. Most people don't have open marriages and never did, but that doesn't mean you can't play the sex-talk game. You probably had experiences with other people before you married. Maybe you even had an affair or two during your marriage. If you feel secure with each other, there's no reason why you can't talk about those experiences. It's selfish to keep the memories to yourself. Share them with your partner. You might be surprised at how sex talk can spice up your sex life.

TELLING TALES

Liz, twenty-nine, is about 5´6˝, with a narrow waist, flat stomach, and ample behind. Her brown hair is short and wavy. A court stenographer, she is dressed in a pale yellow business suit when we meet her. The suit would give her a conservative appearance if she didn't leave the top three jacket buttons undone to reveal the deep furrow of her cleavage. Whenever she moves even slightly, the soft curves of her big round breasts bob into view, making it hard to notice anything else about her.

You want me to talk about sex. Hah, you picked the right person for that. Talking about sex is just about my favorite thing to do, and always has been. You know, it's funny. I get plenty of sex, but I think I like talking about it almost as much as I like doing it.

Explicit erotic conversation has always turned me on. When I was nineteen, I ran with a pretty wild crowd. Everything turned me on back then. My two best friends at the time were Maggie and Sara. We used to get a special kick out of sitting around drinking wine, smoking joints, and talking about the guys we had made it with.

We spent hours describing, in detail, the things they did to us, even comparing the size of their dicks. We were three crazy girls, interested in nothing but sex and drugs and rock and roll. None of us had a steady boyfriend, and we thought our mission in life was to fuck every guy in town. Sometimes, while we were telling each other of our exploits, two of us, or even all three of us, would realize that we'd been screwing the same guy. That made it even more fun.

About five years ago, right around the time I met Kirby, my girlfriends and I started drifting apart. Kirby and I went together for three years before we finally got married, and I didn't see the girls much during that period. I haven't seen Maggie at all since the wedding and Sara only once.

Sex between Kirby and me is superb, and it gets better all the time. We spent lots of time playing with our sexuality, always learning new things about each other. I know exactly where to touch him to make him hard and stiff. He knows all the little places where a gentle kiss can make me quiver. It didn't take him long to find out how much I like talking about sex.

During our love play one night, soon after we started seeing each other, he startled me with a question. We were stretched out naked on the big couch in his apartment. (It's our apartment, now.) One of his hands was toying with my breasts, while his other hand stroked me down below. Suddenly, he placed his lips next to my ear, and in a hoarse whisper, asked, "Did you ever do it with another woman?"

His hands had already gotten me pretty hot, but his question doubled my excitement because it brought me back to one of the most erotic periods of my life. I was quiet for a moment, not sure whether I should tell him the truth. I guess I hesitated a little too long because he saw right through me.

"I thought so," he said, slipping a finger inside me to sample the moisture that had begun flowing. "I thought you had. Now tell me all about it. I'm dying to hear." His finger was working expertly to stir up my excitement. I began to feel a deep warmth flush over me, the same feeling I used to get during my sex talks with Maggie and Sara.

Kirby had met them and knew that they had been my best friends for a while, but he didn't know everything. The thought of telling him about us was turning me on incredibly. I wanted to babble about everything at once, but I took a deep breath and started at the beginning.

* * *

I told him about that first afternoon, when we three girls were hanging out and talking about sex. Maggie had started to describe an experience she had with a cousin of hers who lived in another state. She was a little way into the story when I realized that this cousin was a woman, too. Sara must have figured it out at the same time because she interrupted Maggie by sputtering, "Hey, wait a minute. Are you saying you're a closet lezzie or something?"

"Don't be stupid," Maggie answered. "You know all the guys I've fucked. I'm no lesbian, but sex with other women can be good, too. My cousin wasn't the only one I ever did it with. Don't tell me you've never tried it."

I thought about the games of doctor and nurse that I played with other kids while growing up. At the age of seven or eight, it didn't matter to me whether they were boys or girls. I got just as much of a charge out of it either way, but that didn't mean I was a lesbian. Maybe Maggie had something.

Sara became introspective. In a quiet voice that had a tremor of excitement running through it, she said, "Tell us what you did with her, Maggie. Every single detail."

Maggie said that her cousin, who was a couple of years older than she, was the first to introduce her to girl-girl sex. When she started describing her cousin's breasts, I could see that her memories were arousing her. They were arousing me, too.

She talked about how it felt to touch those breasts for the first time and how erect her cousin's nipples had become when Maggie started petting them. She talked about how it was to put her mouth on them, about what it was like to lick another woman's breasts, to suck on feminine nipples.

My own nipples were so hard by then that they were actually hurting. I had never heard anything so exciting before. My ears pounded so loudly that they almost drowned out Maggie's voice.

She talked about how her cousin undressed her, how it felt to feel her pants and panties being pulled off, and how her cousin had buried her face in Maggie's pussy and licked her up, down, and sideways. She said she came over and over again as her cousin's tongue taught her the delights of female eroticism. Then she said that the best part of all was when she had gone down on her cousin.

I was absolutely fascinated. I heard my own voice asking, "Tell us what that was like."

"I'll do better than that," Maggie said, flashing me an impish grin. "I'll show you."

I didn't understand why the thought of what she was suggesting had me trembling with desire. I did know that it scared the shit out of me. "No, thank you very much. I don't think so," I said. "I'm only curious. I'm not . . . "

"I'm curious, too," Sara said, "so I'm going to watch."

"You're not going to watch *me*," I sputtered, "because I'm not . . . " Before I could say another word, Maggie and Sara jumped me. The three of us started wrestling on the carpet, all laughing and screaming. I struggled a bit, but maybe not as hard as I could have.

At last, Sara pinned me down by lying across my chest and shoulders, while Maggie tugged at my jeans. I'll never forget the way it felt to have her undressing me. It was so exciting that it was terrifying in a way. I was glad she left my panties on. Otherwise, it would have been just too intense.

At this point, Kirby interrupted to ask if I could describe the panties I had worn. I could because I remembered them well. I still remember everything about that afternoon.

The panties were black string bikinis, with enough fabric to almost, but not quite, cover my crack and pubic hair. Maggie began stroking me through them as soon as she finished yanking my jeans down to my ankles and pulling them off my feet. Excitement poured out of me, wetting the panties where she was touching them.

Sara wasn't holding me down any more. She didn't have to. Instead, she was unbuttoning my shirt, undoing my bra, and working them both off my shoulders, with a little cooperation from me. Suddenly, except for the damp little panties, I was completely nude.

My girlfriends knelt on either side of me, both still fully dressed. They began caressing my breasts and rolling my nipples between their fingers. My hips were bumping and grinding, pressing my ass down against the floor and then lifting it high into the air.

Sara reached across me to hold one breast up for Maggie to suck. The feeling of having one woman's hand on my breast while the other's mouth explored its tip was incredible. Then Sara began sucking the other nipple and that felt even better.

Telling it all to Kirby brought the experience back vividly. I felt Maggie's tongue swirling in graceful circles around my swollen nipple and sensitive pink aureole. I felt Sara sucking a little too hard and even biting slightly. The combination of Maggie's practiced strokes and Sara's clumsy explorations made my head spin.

Maggie looked up to be sure I was watching her. Then, without taking her lips from my breast, she reached for Sara's hand and placed it on my crotch. Together they petted me through the soft material of the bikinis. Then, lightly, they started stroking my inner thighs. Each stroke started just above the knee and trailed slowly upward until it reached the puffy panty crotch. They drew the backs of their hands across the sensitive mound before returning to my legs and leaving me to wish silently for their touch on my pussy again.

Finally, when I thought I would not be able to stand the torment any longer, I felt my panties being pulled downward. I looked down, and to my surprise, saw that Sara was now taking the lead. Her fingers tugged at the damp wisp, pulling the waist string over my hips and down my legs. For a long delicious moment, I was aware of nothing but that I was lying absolutely still and totally naked before my two girlfriends. They stood and stared down at me before hastily stripping off their own clothes. They dropped to their knees as soon as they were nude. Each held one of my ankles as they slowly spread my legs apart.

I told Kirby how exciting it was to be displayed so nakedly to the two women, to know that my pussy was wide open to their gaze. I felt them looking at it. Sara's eyes were bright.

"Put your hand here, Sara," Maggie said. "Feel how wet she is." Sara did as Maggie instructed, and I felt the touch of two women's hands on my triangle at the same time. When Maggie held my sex lips apart for Sara to slip a finger inside me, colored strobe lights seemed to go off all around me.

I was reliving it as I described it to Kirby. Sara was fucking me with her finger, while Maggie slowly rolled my clit around in its pool of heated liquid. I felt sex fluids wetting my thighs and the cheeks of my ass, coating the four feminine hands that touched and caressed my hot sex. I was being prepared for something mystical, like a virgin is prepared for sacrifice.

Then the wonderful erotic ritual began. Maggie knelt between my knees and bent forward to place her face at the juncture of my thighs. She blew soft hot kisses against the outer lips, until they parted and turned aside for her. Using just the tip of her tongue, she made deliciously delicate contact with the exposed inner surfaces.

At the same time, Sara's hands slid lightly up over my belly to begin cupping and caressing my breasts. In just a few minutes, she had become an expert. Her touch complimented the soft lapping strokes of Maggie's tongue. The two women watched each other as they did those incredible things to me, and I watched them both.

I described it all to Kirby so he could watch the three of us. I showed him my breasts with Sara's hands on them. I showed him my pussy, open wide for Maggie's mouth. He saw me dig my heels into the carpet to lift myself up against Maggie's face. He saw her hands cup my ass to raise me even higher. And as I narrated it for him, I felt her tongue begin to enter me.

Maggie did things with her mouth that no man had ever been able to do for me. The movements of her tongue and lips blended perfectly with my desire. She understood my sexual need as only another woman could.

My hand lightly fell against Sara's naked hip. Her skin was so soft, so smooth. I began exploring her, touching her breasts and petting the cheeks of her ass. I closed my eyes and tried to picture Maggie's mouth working on me as my hands roamed over Sara's body. When my fingertips discovered the moisture of Sara's sex and felt how different her pussy was from mine, I realized for the first time that no two women are created the same way.

I was just about to penetrate Sara's puckered slit when Maggie took her face from me and moved Sara into her place. Sara immediately started nibbling and nuzzling at my opening, as if she had been doing it all her life. It was so natural, so right. First her tongue slipped inside and then it withdrew to head straight for my clit.

Maggie was on her hands and knees alongside me, her face near Sara's. Her backside was toward me, and I could look right at her pussy. I had never seen another woman's sex so close up before. It was beautiful. The outer lips were a soft delicate pink, and they were all pouty and puffy with desire. The downy little hairs that grew all around her crack curled softly like a furry frame around the center of her womanhood.

Maggie watched intently as Sara licked my swollen button. By now, my clit was so hard, so thick, so big, that it was easy for Sara to place her lips around it to suck ever so gently. I sighed deeply, making sounds of hot sex without any shame or embarrassment.

It seemed so natural for the three of us to enjoy sex together. My two friends were so giving, so eager to please me, that I wanted to do something for them, too. I began stroking Maggie's bottom, letting my fingers trail over her curves as I searched for her pussy. When I encountered the moisture of her sex juices, my body began to tingle. The sensation of having my hand on another woman's sex was almost as exciting as the feeling of another woman's tongue on my most personal spot. It surprised me that I responded this way with other women.

I inserted my finger into Maggie's slit and began twisting it and driving it inside, thinking of how I like my own pussy handled. Sara was sucking on my clit, making me feel things I had never felt before. I couldn't believe it, but I knew an orgasm was beginning. I was actually going to come while my hand was in one woman's pussy and another woman's tongue was on my clit. The feeling was indescribable. All I could tell Kirby was that it was an orgasm I'll remember forever.

Sara understood exactly how much stimulation to give me after my climax ended. She knew exactly when to take her tongue from my sensitive button and begin nuzzling at my pubes. I had been brought to the height of sexual passion, but she was bringing me down to earth again—gradually, easily, in a way only a woman could understand. I just lay there for a while with my eyes closed, slowly catching my breath.

At this point in my story, I became aware that Kirby's breath was coming in short labored pants and that his eyes were glazed with excitement. He was holding his stiff cock in both hands, lightly stroking himself. I watched him, pleased at the effect my story had had. He jerked a little harder when I stopped talking. "Go on," he said. "Don't stop now. I want to hear the rest. Did you do them, too?"

"Yes," I said. "That afternoon, and lots of times after that. Sometimes it was Maggie and Sara and me; sometimes it was just Maggie and me, or Sara and me. We did everything you can possibly imagine, but I'm not going to tell you all of it at once."

I climbed into Kirby's lap and straddled his huge erection. Our lovemaking was fast and frantic. The talk had stimulated both of us, and we came within seconds.

Since then, telling Kirby tales about us three horny young women has become a regular part of our sex play. He loves hearing them, and I love telling them. We both get fantastically turned on when I talk about those days of unashamed experimentation. Our sex is simply marvelous.

My time with Maggie and Sara stands out in my mind as one of the most erotic periods in my life. I'm glad that Kirby likes me to talk about it. I know we girls would never have done the things we did with each other if Kirby, or any other man, had been present, but through my words, he gets to be right there in the room with us. It excites me even more to have him there, reliving the whole thing with me.

5

I SEE YOU

HUMANS LEARN PRIMARILY BY WATCHING OTHERS. HUNGER prompts us to put food in our mouths, but using a fork or a spoon is not a natural behavior. We only find out how to use utensils when we see our parents doing so. It might be instinctive for us to wrap ourselves in something to warm our bodies, but seeing clothes on other people is what teaches us how to dress.

Keeping ourselves alive by eating and staying warm is the most important thing we do. If we didn't, our species would be extinct. Sexually reproducing ourselves is equally important, however. Failing to do that would also lead to extinction.

Although we learn many important functions by watching, we are not usually permitted to observe others having sex. Except when we are actually performing the reproductive act, our culture even forbids looking at the body parts involved in reproduction. Biology will drive us to make sufficient genital contact to ensure propagation of the species, but anything more than that we're supposed to figure out by trial and error.

Probably because of these taboos and prohibitions, many people are driven by an intense desire to see the body parts that are usually hidden from them. Men and women purchase magazines containing nude photos of members of the opposite sex. Television commercials often feature the bodies of attractive models of both genders, wearing as little as the law will permit. Video shops do a brisk business in X-rated movies, showing genuine people engaging in genuine sex.

An interest in seeing the sexual organs or sex acts of others is called "voyeurism." One way or another, it affects us all. If it didn't, those magazines, commercials, and erotic entertainments would not be so prevalent. If the desire to watch weren't so universal, there would not be as many action groups working so hard to suppress it.

No book about erotic turn-ons would be complete without a chapter like this one. Many people told us that they were aroused by seeing or visualizing other people in the nude or having sex. We chose the stories of Barney and Amber because they illustrate four common variations on the voyeuristic theme.

Barney is a classic Peeping Tom. He enjoys surreptitiously looking into the windows of his neighbors, setting up his telescope at night with his own house lights off so he won't be caught. Amber, however, watches openly, and only with the consent of those she is observing.

For Barney, voyeurism seems to be an erotic end in itself. Although looking at the bodies of others arouses him, it is not directly connected with any other sexual activity of his own. Amber observes others while she is engaging in sexual relations. She thus combines voyeurism and exhibitionism with her own active participation.

FAREWELL PERFORMANCE

Barney, fifty-nine, describes himself as a semiretired investor. Although he gets no more specific than that, it is obvious that he enjoys an affluent lifestyle without working too hard at it. He and his wife live in a seaside community located well beyond commuting range from the nearest city. Barney is 5´8˝ and 180 pounds, with a receding hairline. His blue eyes sparkle as he admits that he likes peeking in windows when there is "something worth looking at." He smiles easily and seems to be making fun of himself when talking about his voyeuristic tendencies.

I've always loved the sight of a naked woman. Hey, what man doesn't? But here's the weird thing. I find it much more exciting when I see her through a window. I don't exactly know what it is, but for me, peeking is more of a turn-on than outright looking.

Fortunately, my wife understands. Sometimes, when I'm out working in the garden or something, she'll undress in front of the window so I can spy on her from outside. Boy, let me tell you, that turns me on more than you can imagine. And she knows it! She really understands how I love to peek.

Occasionally, she even watches with me. A while back, we lived in an apartment in an East Coast city. It was a singles neighborhood, and the people who lived in the buildings around us were real casual about leaving their blinds open. Something worth looking at was always going on. When our neighbors had sleepover company, my wife and I would shut our lights and use binoculars to watch them play their bedroom games. It was good entertainment, and most of the time, it led to great sex for us. While we made love, we would be thinking and sometimes even talking about what we had seen through the windows.

Of course, that was some time ago. We don't live in the city anymore, so I don't have quite as much opportunity for peeking, but I still get a look whenever I can. We now live in a resort area. The houses near us are only occupied during the summer, when the owners move in for vacation, or on weekends, when the houses are rented to short-term tenants. Because the ocean views are so gorgeous, many people leave their shades open all the time. So when there are tenants, I can usually count on some interesting peeks.

There are new people to see most weekends, which makes my voyeurism doubly interesting. I find the turnover really exciting, and most of the tenants aren't around long enough to figure out how much can be seen from the neighboring houses—especially from mine.

I always keep a pair of binoculars handy, so if there's anything worth looking at, I usually get a glimpse. I know exactly where the hot tubs are located and which windows give me the best bedroom views. I've become very skillful at predicting where the action is going to take place.

I love to watch women drying themselves and dressing after a shower.

Getting into the bathroom with them without their knowledge is a huge turn-on for me. If I'm lucky enough to catch a peek of a couple making love, that's a real bonus. But that's pretty unusual. Mostly, I get lots of quick shots of naked ladies climbing in and out of hot tubs. Fences around the yards lull them into a false sense of security. They never seem to realize that from my upstairs windows I can see right over those fences.

Just recently, the fellow who owns the house next to mine called me to say that he was renting it to three young women for a two-week stay. He was a little nervous because of their youth. I guess he was afraid they might throw some wild parties. Anyway, he asked me to keep an eye on the place. And, boy, did I.

The women arrived in a van later that afternoon. All three were good-looking. I figured them to be in their early twenties. One, a fleshy brunette with long hair that hung nearly to her ass, wore a loose ankle-length dress. I was watching her through my binoculars as she unloaded the van when the good Lord sent me a gust of wind. It swirled the dress high above her waist, showing me her firm, but plumply rounded, ass in a pair of white cotton panties. She made a token effort to pull the skirt back down as the two other women roared with laughter. Then she gave up and just let the wind do what it wanted with her. I knew I was going to have an exciting couple of weeks.

Besides the brunette, there was a thin blonde. She wore jeans that hugged her narrow hips and a skimpy halter-top that barely covered her little titties. But the third young lady was the one who turned out to be my favorite. She was capped with a head of tight red curls that made me wonder if she had a snatch to match. Obviously bra-less, her huge boobs strained against a tight white T-shirt. I hoped that she would use the front bedroom. It's got a big picture window that allows me a great unobstructed view.

Luck was with me on that one. The redhead did sleep in the front room, and the shade was never closed. But my luck improved even more—all three of the girls ended up using the front bedroom for dressing in after their showers. I took to wearing the binoculars on a strap around my neck so that I was ready for a peek whenever the occasion presented itself.

At night, I would even be so bold as to move my telescope and its tripod to where I could point it directly into the front bedroom window. As long as my lights were out, I knew they wouldn't be able to see me. The telescope is so powerful that it made me feel as if I were standing with my nose pressed right against their window, looking in with no possibility of being caught.

Of course, during the day, I moved the telescope out of their line of sight. The last thing I wanted was to give myself away and bring down the curtain on the wonderful shows they were giving me. Not rated X, exactly, but a pretty strong R.

The show almost turned to X one night when three boys in a red convertible came to visit. I watched them party, drinking beer and wine for quite a while. I really got my hopes up when the three couples separated and headed for different bedrooms. There was bound to be some action, and a good chance I'd get to see it. As soon as the redhead and her friend entered the front bedroom, I brought my telescope into play.

I was rewarded with a clear view of the young couple as they sat on the bed and embraced. When they began undressing each other, I invited my wife to join me for a sizzling performance. I looked through the scope while she used the binoculars.

The redhead had her boyfriend's pants off and was tugging at his shorts. He was busy unbuttoning her shirt to reveal an overflowing bra. He was in the process of unfastening it when she seemed to say something and point to the window. He stopped abruptly and jumped to his feet. To my disappointment, he pulled down the shade and brought the show to a halt.

When I got up the next morning, the convertible was gone and so were the boys. But at least the shades were open again, so I got my regular glimpses of seminaked females moving through the house in various stages of undress. They always seemed to be dressing, undressing, or changing their clothes. I found it hard to concentrate on anything else.

On their second Saturday in the house, it occurred to me that they would probably be leaving the following day. I felt bad about it because I didn't ever remember a time with better peeking. I attribute it to their generation's lack of the Victorian modesty that haunts my own age-group.

Sunday morning, I was up bright and early with my binoculars in hand, gazing into their windows. I didn't exactly set the alarm, but I'm sure that my unconscious clock woke me so that I wouldn't miss my last chance to watch. As it was, they were still sleeping.

I could see the redhead snuggled under a light blanket. True, it shielded her from my view, but its contours suggested the voluptuous curves of her youthful body, and that suggestion was enough to turn me on.

I watched with anticipation as she stirred, just beginning to come out of her sleep. I wondered whether she was nude and nursed the hope that she would throw back the covers to reveal herself in total nakedness. Instead, she moved slowly, stretching her arms high over her head and rubbing the sleep from her eyes.

A moment later, she swung her legs over the side of the bed to search with bare feet for a pair of shaggy slippers. As she emerged from under the blanket, I saw that she was wearing a long T-shirt. It covered most of her, but couldn't hide the roundness of her tits. Through my binoculars, I thought I could even see the outlines of her nipples. When she got up and headed for the bathroom, I watched her muscular butt moving under the shirt.

I was pretty sure I had seen all I was going to see, but of course, I never gave up. While I busied myself making coffee, I repeatedly glanced over, on the odd chance that I would get a final peek of the women getting dressed. The other two didn't interest me as much as the redhead, but I swung my binoculars from window to window anyway.

I got a good look at Blondie in the kitchen. She must have just woken up, too, because she was still wearing her nightgown. It was a shortie and real sheer. Instead of hiding the view, it improved it. I could see the triangular shadow of her pubic hair and the firm little cones of her breasts with their tiny pink nipples peering through.

The brunette walked into the room, wrapped in two towels. One was wound around the long wet hair she had piled on her head. The other covered her body from just under the arms to midthighs and was held in place by a twist at the top. While she was reaching for something on the table, the blonde came up behind her and playfully yanked at the towel, causing it to fall to the floor. They both laughed and whacked each other's asses a couple of times before picking it up.

I don't know what happened after that, because I noticed the redhead reentering her bedroom at that very moment. I turned the binoculars back to her window. She was wearing absolutely nothing.

I had a rush of mixed feelings. I was overjoyed at my good fortune, and at the same time, cursed the bad luck that gave me the best view of all on the day of their departure. Just when I had learned enough about their routine to catch all the sights, they were taking off. I pushed my thoughts aside, to make the most of the little time I had left. I focused my binoculars on the redhead's nudity.

Before, she had always walked briskly, so that even when I got to see her, it was only for a flash. But that last day, her movements seemed slow and deliberate. I watched her walk to the dresser and fiddle with the radio. A moment later, her naked body started swaying rhythmically, obviously dancing to music that she could hear but I couldn't. She was directly in front of the window with her back to me, her whole body undulating, her ass rotating in circles. She shuffled her feet and raised her arms in the air, as though performing for an imaginary audience. Slowly, she turned a full 360 degrees in place, giving me a long thorough look at every part of her.

My hands holding the binoculars trembled with that weird anticipation I get when I'm seeing something good and hoping for something better. When she had turned completely around and her back was to me again, I went for the telescope. I knew it was risky because if she saw it, I'd be caught and my show would end. But I couldn't resist. This performance I just had to see up close.

I walked backwards so I wouldn't have to tear my eyes from the window. As quickly as I could, I dragged the scope into position. It only took a moment to aim and focus, but it seemed like an hour. When I finally got to look through it, I saw that she had placed an open suitcase on the bed. Her body was still moving sensuously to the music as she danced back and forth across the room, taking things out of the closet and drawers to place them in the suitcase.

When she bent over to reach for something, that telescope brought me right up next to her naked ass. It was round and full without being fat. I swear she looked like a *Playboy* centerfold. I studied her as she straightened, enjoying the sight of her trim waist and wide flaring hips. Her bottom humped forward and back to the beat of the music.

I knew she was going to turn around, any second, to walk back to the suitcase. I was torn. I didn't want to miss the opportunity of seeing her stark naked, full front, but I didn't want her to spot the scope either. Before I had a chance to make a decision, it was done. She whirled, still gyrating, and faced me full on. Her eyes might have been closed. I'm not sure. In any event, she didn't appear to see me.

She shook her shoulders, making her big tits swing from side to side. I stared through the eyepiece at the thick red nipples as they inscribed a series of arcs in the air. Then I focused lower, filling the lens with her thick patch of red pubic hair. It seemed to go on forever, sprawling across the bottom of her white belly and spilling over onto her creamy thighs. No bikini wax for this red-haired beauty.

I couldn't believe my good fortune. She was really performing, her hips thrusting back and forth like a dancer in a strip joint, but I was the only one in the audience, and she didn't even know I was there. I watched her making the exact same motions a person would make while screwing. I could feel myself getting hard.

I wanted to wake up my wife so she could enjoy the show with me, but I just couldn't bring myself to move away from this erotic performance. I was so aroused that I felt the pre-come oozing, the way it sometimes happens when you're really turned on.

The lady continued to dance, sometimes bending to put something in the suitcase, sometimes reaching above her head to retrieve something from the closet shelf. She was dealing with one item at a time, so each piece that she placed in the bag involved another trip across the room. Boy, let me tell you, I was in heaven.

She was moving so slowly that I swear if I had a more powerful telescope, I would have been able to count her pubic hairs. She almost looked like she was counting them herself. She stood by the bed, directly in front of the window, looking down and running her fingers through that dense red jungle. I thought, Is this a dream or what?

But, wait, it got even better. She lifted a foot and placed it on the bed, reaching down with one hand to stroke herself between the legs. Slowly, she caressed her own thighs and pussy. With her other hand, she started petting her tits, doing things I could only imagine to the nipples with her fingers. Her head was moving in little circles.

Whenever I thought her eyes might be focusing in my direction, I tried to scramble out of her view. The trouble was that if she couldn't see me, I wouldn't be able to see her either. So I never got completely out of the way, but I tried not to be too careless.

I thought I could see one of her fingers plunging in and out of her and rubbing her little love button. Maybe my imagination was just filling in the blanks. Anyway, for quite a while, she gave me the greatest show I ever had as she stood there diddling herself. Eventually, her movements slowed. She abandoned her crotch to stroke her whole body idly, from top to bottom. Once again she stood with both feet on the floor and turned to watch herself in the mirror.

After a minute or so of this, she returned to the suitcase, placing herself directly in front of the window. She leaned over to select a wispy little garment and then held it up in front of the window as if she were studying it in the sunlight while deciding whether to wear it or not. At the same time, she was displaying it to me.

As she stretched the lacy red waistband, I realized that the scrap of cloth was a pair of very brief panties. I guess they met with her approval because, holding them in both hands, she bent forward and lifted one foot into them, then the other. I felt my temperature rise as she pulled the tight panties up over her shapely legs and settled them around her full butt. The waistband stretched across her flat belly a good two inches below the navel.

She patted her backside and looked into the mirror, giving her hips a little shake and turning to show me her lace-covered bottom. Then, returning to the suitcase, she retrieved a matching red bra. She repeated the sunlight stunt, holding the sexy garment up in front of the window for a moment and giving me a good look at it.

I held my breath as she worked her breasts into it, her fingers lingering over the big swollen nipples. The same way I was seizing my final opportunity to peek at her, she seemed to be taking advantage of this last chance to caress herself before she finished dressing. After hooking the snaps, she bent forward at the waist, facing the window. Pulling the bra away from her chest, she gave her boobs a little shake to settle them comfortably inside the cups.

She turned again to look in the mirror, so I got to see her from both sides. Boy, let me tell you, the red lace against her soft youthful skin was a very stimulating sight for me. But the show couldn't last forever. She returned to the suitcase, removed a long knit dress, and quickly slipped it on over her head.

Turning her back to me again, she reached for the tab of the zipper, which was open to the top of her ass. Slowly, she drew it up, gradually covering her smooth white back. Finally, even the red lace of her bra strap was hidden from view by the zipped dress, and the reverse striptease was over.

When she quickly turned to face me again, I didn't even bother to move out of her view. She reached up to close the shade, but her hand stopped for an instant in the middle of its movement. She looked me right in the eye and blew me a little kiss, and I swear, she even made a little bow before the shade came down.

A moment later, all three of the girls came through the front door carrying their bags. In minutes, their van was loaded, and they were pulling it out of the driveway. By then, I was aching with desire.

Before they had driven completely out of view, I had crawled into bed next to my wife. I woke her by entering her from behind. She accepted me with a sleepy, but passionate, moan. We spent the rest of the day making love. Between climaxes, I told her all about our neighbor's farewell performance. It kept us both turned on for hours.

SAME-ROOM SEX

Amber is forty-two, with a compact dancer's body that would be the envy of most twenty-year-olds. Her smooth skin, crystal blue eyes, and long auburn hair shine with the luster of sparkling health. She says she has worked at staying fit since her midteens by maintaining a daily routine of yoga exercises, followed by a five-mile jog and an hour of aerobic dancing. As she speaks, she moves about the room with boundless energy, never once sitting down.

The most exciting thing of all is having sex in the same room with another couple and watching them have sex at the same time. It's such a turn-on that even saying it gives me the shivers. Ivan loves it, too.

It was Ivan who taught me the special excitement of looking at naked bodies. All kinds—big ones, small ones, fat ones, skinny ones, men and women. When somebody is in good physical condition, appreciating their beauty can be a high art, but flabby bodies can be beautiful, too. Ivan says even the ugly ones are beautiful, and I totally agree with him.

I doubt if I ever would have realized how arousing the sight of another naked person can be if I hadn't met Ivan. Until then, I was more interested in having people look at me. Probably, that's why I became a dancer. When I'm on stage, dancing in front of an audience, I know their eyes are on my body, watching every move I make. I take pride in my body, so I keep it fit, firm, and properly fueled.

Years ago, when it was in to redo all that old stuff from the seventies, I played one of the street girls in an off-Broadway production of

Hair. At the finale, the entire cast comes out on stage, and everybody takes their clothes off. It's been a tradition ever since *Hair* was a smash hit on Broadway.

Part of the tradition is that cast members don't have to take anything off at all unless they feel like it at that very moment. Most of the dancers got into it to some extent, but some nights more than others. I stripped all the way every single time. I just loved to feel the audience looking at me in the raw. I'll never try to deny that it turned me on.

I met Ivan shortly after that production closed. (I'm not going to tell you how long ago it was.) After a long round of off-Broadway and off-off-off-Broadway, I was auditioning for a Broadway chorus for the very first time. Ivan was one of the investors. He backs lots of shows, just as a hobby.

I had heard of him, and some of the other girls in the line had actually met him. They said he was filthy rich and lived a fast affluent life. Women were always throwing themselves at him because he had a reputation for spending money easily and showing them a good time. They called him Ivan the Great and bragged to each other about having been in his bed.

When I first saw him, he was sitting in the front row next to the director and choreographer, watching the audition and making suggestions about who should stay and who should be cut. At the end of the afternoon, I was still in the running and was instructed to return the next morning. As I was getting my things together to leave, Ivan the Great himself approached me and asked if I'd have dinner with him.

He was about fifteen years older than I. And cocky! Something about his overly assertive attitude made me feel like putting him in his place. So, even though I very much wanted to accept his invitation, I heard my mouth spitting a curt no at him.

My refusal hit him like a spray of ice water. He just stared at me with a thinly disguised expression of shock for what seemed an eternity. Then he turned on his heel and hurriedly walked out of the theater.

The next morning, I was afraid that he might have bumped me from the chorus, but the director told me I was definitely in. Ivan wasn't even there. I didn't admit it to myself at the time, but I was disappointed when I searched the theater with my eyes and couldn't find him.

I didn't see him again until the end of the first week's rehearsal. I happened to glance toward the back of the theater and noticed him sitting alone. A moment later, when the stage director called a ten-minute break, Ivan got out of his seat and walked briskly toward the stage. I watched him come up the stage steps and walk straight to where I was standing talking to one of the other dancers.

Addressing her, Ivan said, "Will you excuse us, please?" Even if she hadn't known who he was, the authority in his voice would have made her obey. She faded, without a word. Turning to me, he said, "Amber, I just came to let you know that we're having dinner tonight. I have your address. My car will be there at eight." He didn't wait for an answer, because he hadn't asked a question. He just turned and left. I wouldn't have had time to refuse if I had wanted to. That didn't matter, though, because I hadn't wanted to.

Later that evening, we wined and dined at a restaurant that very few New Yorkers have ever heard of, let alone been inside. The waiters all acted as though Ivan were the president of the United States. They never asked what he wanted, and he didn't have to order. They brought one marvelous dish after another and poured wine from bottles so old that the labels had started turning yellow.

After the meal, we lingered over brandy and coffee for more than an hour, getting acquainted. His earlier cocky attitude was gone. Ivan was positively charming. There was something so sexy about his manner that I found myself getting a little turned on thinking about what might be coming later.

When we were done, no bill was presented, no credit card was imprinted, no signature was taken. Ivan just nodded to the maitre d' and we left. His car was already at the curb, the chauffeur poised to open the door for us.

Without waiting for instructions, the driver pulled the car into Manhattan's traffic. We continued the conversation we had begun at the restaurant, and I didn't pay much attention to where we were going. I was surprised when the car stopped and I noticed we were in front of my own apartment.

The chauffeur opened the car door for me and assisted me out. Ivan got out as well and accompanied me to the front door. I thought about how messy my place was and wondered how he would react to it, but he made no attempt to come inside. Instead, he asked if I would join him for breakfast the following morning.

"I have to be at the theater for rehearsal at eight A.M.," I said.

"Then I'll pick you up at six," he answered. Taking my hand, he brought it to his lips and brushed it gently. "Thank you for a lovely evening." That was supposed to be my line. He had taken the words right out of my mouth.

That night, I thought about how different he was from everything I had heard about him. I was sure that the stories had all been false or at least exaggerations. Weeks later, he confessed that all the rumors were true, but that he acted differently with me because he had fallen in love that first time I turned him down.

We dated for more than a month before we ever had sex. When we did, it was marvelous. After we made love the first time, I started spending several nights a week in Ivan's luxury penthouse, which had a view that overlooked the entire world. When our relationship had become intimate, he let me in on what he called his special personal tic. Ivan liked going to sex parties. I had heard about them before, but had no idea they were so common in the world we both inhabited. Ivan told me about a group of show people and investors who got together frequently to have wild orgies that lasted far into the night. He asked if I'd like to go with him, assuring me that we would only watch.

Naturally, I accepted. At the very least, my curiosity had to be satisfied. Besides that, I was intrigued at the thought of people having sex right out in the open, where other people could watch them. I had never seen other people having sex, and the idea was very arousing.

The first party he took me to was in a very high class West Side condominium, near where John Lennon had lived. I recognized a few of the people from the theater scene, but nobody I really knew. That made it a little easier.

An ordinary cocktail party was going on in the living room, but people were leaving in groups of three, or four, or even more, to head for the apartment's many bedrooms. In a whisper, Ivan said, "They're going off to have sex. Shall we watch some of them?"

He led me from one room to another, where we watched people coupling in every possible combination. It overwhelmed me at first, but it excited me tremendously. I stood open-mouthed, staring as people mounted each other at random. I saw men with other men and women with other women. I saw mixed groups forming daisy chains, with each participant making sexual contact with at least two others.

After watching for two or three hours, we returned to Ivan's place, where we made love until the sun came up. Ivan had introduced me to a new world of sexual stimulation. As he rolled me in his arms, I pictured the bodies I had seen, the sex organs, the couplings. I had orgasm after orgasm as he made passionate love to me, using his hands and his mouth and his wonderful penis in a million creative ways. Watching had aroused him even even more than it did me.

From then on, we attended sex parties regularly, always observing the action from the sidelines and returning to the penthouse for incredibly exquisite sex afterwards. I was reaching heights of excitement that I never knew existed. Any sexual inhibitions I ever had were quickly melting away.

I thought of how exciting it had been to take my clothes off on the stage. Being nude before an audience was a thrill I never forgot. I wondered how it would be to have people standing by, watching Ivan and me making love. One night, after a party and while we were immersed in the throes of passion, I asked if he'd be willing to try it.

He was quiet for a moment. "I've joined in the orgies before," he admitted, "but with women who didn't mean anything to me. I didn't mind sharing them. I even got off on watching as other men pawed at them and gnawed at them, but I don't want anyone else touching you. You're mine."

His words made me feel proud. By now I was very much in love with him, and I was pleased that he thought of me as his. We decided that at the next party we would make love publicly, but that we would not allow anyone else to enter our little world.

It didn't work out that way, however. We went into a bedroom where the floor was littered with people connected to each other by their sex organs. We found an empty bed and lay down on it after undressing each other quickly. I liked the feeling I got when I saw people looking at us, studying my nudity and Ivan's with their open glances. They watched my nipples getting hard and that made my nipples even harder.

We were usually watchers, so when we lay down together and began caressing each other's bodies, we attracted the attention of those we usually watched. A man and woman sat on the edge of the bed, rubbing each other's genitals and staring as Ivan entered me. The feeling was unbelievable. We were totally on display, showing our sex to the world while watching the incredible performances going on all around us.

Then the man who was sitting on the bed spoiled everything by touching one of my breasts. I felt Ivan's body stiffen and his manhood go limp inside me. I pushed at the man's hand until he got the point and returned to his own partner. Ivan pressed his loins against me in a desperate effort to overcome his loss of emotional control, but the mood was broken. We dressed and went home, a little less stimulated than usual.

We tried again at another party. This time, a woman who had drunk too much insisted on rubbing Ivan's penis and kept trying to suck my breasts. We left early, realizing this was not going to work for us.

Later, at home, Ivan said he had an idea. He liked the thought of having others watch us almost as much as he liked watching them. Parties obviously were not the best way of going about it, but meeting on a personal level with people we knew from the parties might be the answer. There were a few couples we especially liked, and maybe we could get together with one them privately, just two couples sharing intimate moments. Each person would make love to his or her partner only, but the four of us would be in the same room, watching each other.

Ivan was a man of action, through and through. He made the arrangements the very next day. That night Alice and Leonard joined us for brandy. After we sat in the living room for a short time, drinking and chatting, Ivan said, "Amber and I are going into the other room. Would you care to join us?"

The four of us went to the bedroom, where Ivan and I sat on the bed while Alice and Leonard settled down on the sofa. There was a delicious feeling of perversion in the air. It was just the four of us, and it was so easy.

Alice began removing her clothes immediately, her partner's hands roaming over each part of her body as she exposed it. He cupped her breasts in his hands and held them up for Ivan and me to see. He pushed her legs apart and showed us the dark shadow of her sex. All the while, Alice was opening his buttons and unzipping his fly. Soon he, too, was naked.

Ivan took me in his arms just as Alice began licking Leonard's nipples. We undressed quickly, a sense of desperation coming over us. Ivan's penis seemed much bigger than usual. I know my vagina was wetter. We stroked and petted each other without ever tearing our eyes from the sight of what our friends were doing to one another with their tongues and mouths.

We became intoxicated by the acts we were witnessing. It was the turn-on of a lifetime. I wanted to show the other couple something as exciting as they were showing us. I wanted them to see all of me. I wanted them to see how beautiful it was when Ivan entered me.

I lay on my back, opening myself to their view. They were watching as their bodies came together. Ivan crept between my legs. Alice and Leonard stopped moving, frozen in an erotic tableau as they waited, breathless, for us to combine. I lightly touched Ivan's penis with the tips of my fingers, aiming it at my waiting orifice. When he slid inside me, all four of us groaned.

Ivan and I began the steady rhythm of intercourse. Alice and Leonard imitated our movements, doing with their bodies everything that we were doing with ours. Each of us looked from one to the other, experiencing a perverse thrill at watching others have sex while feeling precisely what they were feeling.

Alice had Leonard inside her. I had Ivan inside me. As Leonard pumped in and out of her, I felt Ivan pumping in and out of me. As Alice fastened her eyes to the sight of Ivan's penis in my vagina, I fastened mine on the sight of Leonard's penis in hers. I knew what her body was feeling, and I knew the excitement her mind experienced.

Ivan whispered in my ear, describing Alice's breasts to me, painting a word picture of Leonard's swinging scrotum. "Tell them, too," I gasped. I was so aroused that I was struggling for breath. "Tell them what you see."

Ivan spoke louder, composing an impromptu erotic ode to the couple making love on the sofa. Then, using words of the gutter in a way that made my skin tingle, Alice spoke in smutty detail of the way Ivan's penis looked as it parted the tissues of my vulva. Leonard's turn was next, and then mine. For hours, we exchanged erotic descriptions as we showed each other and watched each other perform dramatic feats of sex.

During one of Ivan's orgasms, he announced in rhythmic cries that he was filling me with his seed. A few minutes later, Leonard withdrew from Alice so that we could see his climax erupt. We kept it up most of the night, each couple stimulated by what they saw the other couple doing. Just before dawn, all four of us fell asleep.

Since then, Ivan and I have had many private sessions with other couples. Watching them make love while they watch us has become such an immense turn-on that it carries over into our private moments, too. For days before a get-together, we anticipate the meeting with mounting excitement. We talk about it and think about it. Sometimes, we even plan our sex scenes. Alone in our room, performing intimate acts for no eyes but our own, we turn ourselves on by imagining that we are watching another couple on the sofa.

6

SEX AT WORK

NOT LONG AGO, A WRITER NAMED STUDS TERKEL PUBLISHED
a book entitled *Working,* which consists of a series of interviews conducted by the author with Americans from every walk of life. The people in Terkel's book talk about their jobs. They describe the kinds of tasks they are required to perform and how they feel about their work. Some dislike their jobs; some like them. A few even claim to love their work. The chances are, however, that none enjoys his or her occupation as much as the people whose stories are told in this chapter.

Somehow Terkel missed the people who regard their work as a sexual turn-on. We found quite a few. Others found us. We were a little surprised at how frequently people said that they associate erotic thoughts with their occupations or jobs. We received so many responses that we divided the stories into three categories, each of which is represented in this chapter.

Sometimes the erotic response occurs because the work itself is of a sexual nature. Kathy, a massage therapist, finds that seeing and touching a nude client often has the natural effect of arousing her. She endeavors to hide this from the client, relieving her sexual tension only within the confines of her relationship with her mate.

Even people with jobs that have no direct connection with sex are able to find sexy aspects to them. Jack told us that, while reading residential meters for an electrical company, he has a semierection most of the day because of the possibility that he will see a partially undressed woman. When it happens, he attempts to maintain a professional attitude and is careful to appear uninterested. He rarely has an actual sexual encounter while working.

We encountered a small group of people for whom the nature of the job does not matter at all. What turns them on is the idea of having sex right in the workplace. Their jobs provide the opportunity; their work serves as a kind of foreplay. Jenny calls her employment as a temporary office worker the "ultimate sexual challenge."

MASSAGE THERAPY

Kathy, twenty-seven, is about 5'4" inches. Her arms and shoulders are muscular, her breasts are full and round; however, her waist is narrow and her shapely legs are thin. Her blue-grey eyes shine with pride when she says that the strength of her upper body is the result of her occupation. "You'd be surprised at how my work keeps me in shape," she says, "especially carrying that portable table." Kathy isn't complaining, though. She says her work as a massage therapist provides her greatest turn-on.

I was brought up to believe that I ought to have a profession, so I started college as a science major. I wasn't sure what I would do with a science degree, but I had always been interested in biology and the human body, and science seemed to be the only thing for me to study. It was a kind of knee-jerk reaction. All I knew was that I was supposed to go to school.

It didn't take me long to realize that college wasn't for me. The idea of spending the next five or ten years studying for some vague academic profession just didn't appeal to me. I wanted to get started on my life, so after my first year, I dropped out of college and enrolled in courses at a massage school. Within six months, I had my profession. I was a licensed massage therapist.

I didn't waste time looking for a job. I went right into business for myself. I decided to run ads in a few local newspapers, but when I saw how many other massage therapists were competing for business, I realized I had to come up with some kind of marketing gimmick.

I offered a free fifteen-minute in-home introductory massage, and my phone practically rang off the wall. For the first few weeks, even though I gave lots of massages, I didn't make a dime. I had begun to wonder if my gimmick had been such a good idea after all, but about eighty percent of those freebies have ended up becoming regular clients, so it has turned out great for me.

When Roger and I moved in together about two years ago, he was uptight about my business. He said he didn't like the idea that I made my living going into men's homes and rubbing their naked bodies. I thought that was a rather crude way to put it. We struggled with it for a while, until finally, I got him to see the light.

After all, I had been working at my profession for three years before I even met him. Lots of my clients were women, anyway. As to the men, the fact that I worked only in the client's home—no hotels, nobody coming to my place—kept the perverts away. Also, the person isn't always naked. It's true that I prefer to work without draping the client, but I let them keep their underwear on if they want to, and most of the men choose to do so. It's all very legitimate.

Massage has gotten a bad reputation because of all those so-called massage parlors that are really just fronts for prostitition. Real massage is a respectable art that goes back thousands of years. I'm proud of what I do, and I do it well. Aside from being lucrative, massage therapy is emotionally rewarding. Also, to be honest with you, for me it's the greatest turn-on in the world.

What really convinced Roger was the money. He's still in graduate school, just a year or so away from his Ph.D. He has a fellowship, but it really doesn't pay much, making the financial benefits of my business hard to resist. Besides, he's beginning to realize there are other benefits, too. Nothing else has ever aroused me quite as much as the work I do.

I'm very professional about my work. When the clients are undressing, I always leave the room so they can have privacy. I avoid conversations about the client's or my own personal life. I'm especially careful not to touch any of those places the instructors at the massage school called the no-trespassing zones.

But I must admit that when I'm working on a man—especially if he's the athletic type, someone who takes real good care of himself and has an attractive hard body—I find it a little more interesting than the instructors said we should. While I wait for him to undress, I sometimes catch myself hoping that he will choose to take the underwear off. When I walk back into the room, my eyes involuntarily go straight to the buns, to see whether they're covered or not. When they aren't, I get a peculiar warm feeling.

I always start with the client lying face down on the table. I do the head first, using circular strokes on the scalp to ease away thought-tensions. Then I work the neck and shoulders. You can tell a lot about a person's lifestyle from his neck and shoulders. When I find tense spots, I press my fingertips deep into the muscle and try working them out.

There's something about touching and stroking a strong man's muscles that gets to me. While my hands trace the lines of each individual muscle, I find myself tingling just a little between the legs. It's nice to feel aroused while doing my work. At first, it's an unobtrusive kind of arousal, but as I work my way down his back, it intensifies. When I work on the butt, the gentle arousal sometimes becomes a burning excitement.

It's important to do the buttocks deeply and thoroughly because most of the muscles that move our legs pass through them. Since most people spend most of their work day sitting, those muscles don't usually get properly stretched. If you don't stretch and relax them during the massage, you really haven't done your job.

So I knead and I squeeze those tense gluteus maxima—what you might call the cheeks—until all the client's tension is gone. But mine isn't because by then, my body starts to feel like it's on fire.

Next I work the thighs and legs. Sometimes, getting away from the butt gives me a chance to cool down, but it all depends on the way he's lying. To do a proper job on the thighs, I've got to spread his legs a little. Usually, if he hasn't already assumed the correct position, I hold his ankles and pull them gently apart.

When he's not wearing underwear, some of the sights I see at this point are sexually interesting. I like to see the back of his scrotum, for example. Whether I like it or not, I like it, if you know what I mean. I can't help it. It turns me on.

The most difficult part is when I finish the posterior massage and it's time for the client to turn over onto his back. No matter who or how old he might be, I've never yet had a male client who didn't have at least the beginning of an erection when he turned over. The new clients get embarrassed about it, and I find that a little exciting also. I've learned I can usually put them at their ease by saying something like, "I'm glad you like the massage. Don't worry about your body's responses. They're perfectly natural."

I'd never let any of them know this, but I'll tell you, I find it very exciting to see a man's penis becoming erect a little bit at a time. As I work on the front of their bodies, they sometimes get fully erect. I don't let them see me looking, but as I move around the table, I get to see the erection from all different angles.

Some men have breasts as sensitive as a woman's, so when I rub their chests, I can also see their nipples hardening with excitement. I don't usually touch the nipple itself, but when my fingers swirl around its circumference, I can feel my own nipples getting hard. I always wear an industrial-strength bra so the client won't be able to see the effect the massage is having on me.

When I stroke downward across the rib cage and belly, I stop just at the top of the pubic hair. The hairy parts of the body are usually the most sensitive, you know. With some men, even the slightest contact with the pubic hair makes their penises twitch. Since it's legitimate to look toward my hands as I work, I have a good excuse to observe their erections at that point. Hey, look, as professional as I am, I'm also human. There are times my panties get quite wet while I'm giving a massage.

When I start kneading and stroking the fronts of their thighs, my hands have to come pretty close to their genitals. A good massage gets as close as possible without actually making contact. When I work my way up from the knee, I always stop just at the crease where the thigh joins the torso.

Once in a while—and I assure you, it's never on purpose. Never! I mean that. Once in a while, the backs of my fingers accidentally brush against the scrotum. It happens. It can't always be helped. That's when the fireworks really start for both of us. His penis jumps and bounces, and the sight of it makes me so hot that all I can think of is finishing the massage and getting home to Roger.

But after a massage, the client is supposed to be relaxed, not more tense than he was before it began, so I always finish by working my way down his legs and spending the last five minutes on his feet. By the time I finish the cross strokes on his soles and heels, all the stiffness in his body is gone, including the erection.

My excitement hasn't gone away, though. It's likely to be at a peak. I pack up my table and hurry to the car. If I'm lucky, I don't have to rush off to another appointment. Then I go straight home. Roger is usually there, working away at his computer. When he recognizes my glow, he's more than willing to stop what he's doing and make passionate love to me.

At first, I was worried that he would be upset if he knew what had gotten me so aroused, but we've talked about it, and he really doesn't mind. He says he likes it when I come home wet. He says that even though he loves his work, he wishes it could turn him on the way mine does.

I owe a lot to my occupation. Learning about the body has taught me a lot about mine. If I had not become a massage therapist, I don't think I ever would have experienced the heights of excitement that I do now.

METER READER

Jack, thirty-one and single, is one hundred percent New York City. He says he was born and raised there and can't think of any other place on earth where he'd be willing to live. Flashing a broad smile and a row of dazzling teeth, he adds sar-

donically that he's never really been anyplace else anyway. Jack is about 5´11˝,
with narrow shoulders and a slim waist. His dark hair and eyes blend with his
olive skin. His manner is so warm and friendly that when he matter-of-factly says
that he gets his good looks from his Sicilian mother and his sex appeal from his
Neapolitan father, there isn't a trace of conceit in the statement.

What turns me on? That's a good question. Lots of things do, but I
guess you might say that my job turns me on the most. I just love the
work I do. Sometimes I wake up with a hard-on, just thinking about
going to work.

What I do for a living is, I read electric meters. Maybe it doesn't
sound like a sexy job to you, but you don't know what I know. Nowadays, they put the electric meters outside the house, but this is an old
city, and most of the buildings in my district have been around for a
while. In those days, they put the meters inside, usually in the cellar.

That means that I've got to go in to read them, and so I usually get
to meet the lady of the house once a month. Only for three, four minutes, which may not sound like much to you. But you'd be surprised at
what I get to see in three, four minutes. Maybe five.

Especially in the morning. If anything's going to happen, that's when
it's most likely. See, I start knocking on doors at nine A.M. In some of
those neighborhoods, the ladies are just about turning over in bed
around that time. So when they hear that knock they get all shook up
and come to the door in whatever it is they were sleeping in, with their
hair messed up and no makeup. I love it. If they were sleeping in the
nude, they might just throw on a robe or something.

Usually, the first time I stop by, they get real annoyed and say something like, "Can't you come back later on?"

I just smile, turn on my Italian charm, and act like it's no big deal.
"Sorry to disturb you," I say, "but if you just let me into the cellar, I'll
be out of here before you know it and then you can go back to bed."
I'm real careful not to look at them in a way that makes them uncom-
fortable or anything. I act like seeing a half-dressed woman is just part
of the job.

After a few months, they start thinking of me as an old friend or a member of the family, and they get a lot more casual about the way they come to the door. You'd be surprised at what a lady is likely to show to a member of the family.

Just yesterday, one of the best looking women in my territory came to the door wearing nothing but a towel. It wasn't quite big enough to do the job, either. Oh, it covered her up in front all right, but when she turned around to lead me to the cellar door, it was wide open in back, giving me a full-on view of her tush. I think she knew it, too. But, like I said, she probably thinks of me as family.

I think some of them know very well when I'm coming and dress up special for the occasion, or maybe I should say undress. They open the door in something that's obviously designed to uncover more than it covers. You know, the kind of seducer outfit they get out of a Frederick's catalog and then discover that hubby doesn't even notice, so they wear it for me.

They pull the door open wide, and when I walk in, they put on a whole show of being flustered and acting like they were expecting someone else. I take it in stride and say something like, "Well, Mrs. Whatever, don't you look beautiful." I try to make it sound like something a member of the family would say, but it gives me an excuse to take a real good look. These ladies like to be looked at, and as long as I don't behave in a threatening manner, they feel safe. It's sort of flirting in reverse, and I'm real good at it.

I really like it when I can see the women's bodies reacting to my look. Sometimes, they'll be wearing something sheer that shows the titties, and when I look at them and compliment the outfit, I'll be able to see the nipples getting hard. Of course, I act like I don't even notice, which is what makes it OK.

It's like a game. The rules are that neither of us are allowed to admit that we're playing it. They're giving me an eyeful, and I'm digging every second of it, but we both got to act like nothing is happening. After all, I'm only inside for a couple of minutes. They figure no harm done if I get to see something because I'm in and out and not part of their regular lives.

Most of the time that's as far as it goes, and most of the time that's good enough for me. I go from house to house with a semi hard-on because there's always the chance I'll see some skin. So my work is my turn-on. I got enough sense not to ruin it by getting out of line. I just enjoy what they show me, and I never say or do anything I shouldn't.

There's one lady who really gets me going. She happens to be married to a pretty important politician, so I'll just call her Mrs. X. This Mrs. X, she's in her forties, but she looks absolutely great, spends a lot of money on her hair and nails and clothes. I guess she's got to be the soul of discretion at cocktail parties and all those political functions. That must be rough on her because I happen to know that inside she's a tiger.

Here's how I happen to know that. The very first time I went to read her meter, she came to the door in a shortie nightgown that barely covered the good stuff. Besides coming just to the tops of her thighs, it was completely see-through. She had big dark disks around her nipples, and it was all I could do to keep myself from staring at them.

Instead of going through the flustered routine, she just opened the door wide and casually said, "Come on in." I hadn't even told her yet why I was there.

Suddenly, I was the flustered one. "Just came to read the meter," I mumbled, looking at the floor.

"Well, read it then," she said. "It's down those stairs." I walked past her and when I was about halfway down the steps, she called out, "I'm sure you can find it."

At the sound of her voice, I automatically turned and glanced up to where she was standing at the top of the stairs. I found myself looking straight up the skirt of her nightie. She didn't have anything underneath it, except the coat of fur that nature gave her.

I could see from the sly little smile she wore that she had arranged for me to get the view. My eyes lingered for about three hours—really just a second or two—and then she disappeared, stepping back out of the doorway. I went ahead and did my job, and when I came back up the stairs, she was nowhere in sight. "Thanks, Mrs. X," I hollered. "See you next month."

"Yeah," she answered from some other room. "Next month."

The next time I was scheduled to read her meter, I felt nervous and extra excited all morning. I was pretty sure the first time had just been a fluke—right place, right time sort of thing—and that I wouldn't get lucky again, but there was always the chance.

That time when I knocked, she asked me to wait a moment. It took a good couple of minutes before she finally opened the door, and when she did, she was wearing a black satin robe. It was pretty obvious that she had nothing on underneath. At first, I figured she had covered herself with it after she heard me knocking, but looking back on how long it took her to come back to the door, I think maybe she was dressed when I got there and used the time to take off whatever she was wearing—uncover herself, rather than cover herself.

Anyway, the robe flopped open more than once as she was letting me in and leading me to the cellar steps. Each time it did, I got a good clear look at her curves. First her nice round tits and then the white skin of her belly and hips. When the robe opened, she would close it again with her hands. She didn't seem to be in any rush to block the view, though. I was pretty sure she was deliberately putting on a show and wouldn't mind in the least if I stared right at her, but I still thought I better play it safe, so I did my usual thing of keeping things real casual and keeping my looking as discreet as I could.

After that, I knew that Mrs. X would always give me a show when I went to read her meter. Thinking about it kept me turned on real good. When I got my schedule at the beginning of each month, I would look right away to see when I was supposed to go to her place. Sometimes, I'd think about it for a couple of days in advance, getting myself all hot and hard while driving from one street to the next.

Then one month I got a real surprise. I knocked on her door as usual, dying to see what she'd be wearing for me this time. I wasn't disappointed. When she opened the door, she had on nothing but a brief red bra and panties. The panties were the kind they call tap pants, with like a little skirt attached. Very sexy. The bra was lacy and low-cut—the push-up kind—with those big soft tits of hers practically popping out.

By then, we understood each other well enough that I didn't have to pretend I wasn't interested. As I stepped in, I took a good long look and smiled appreciatively. "Very nice," I said. "Very, very nice."

"Thank you," she answered. "I put it on especially for you because I want you to do me a favor. There's something I need for you to look at in the other room."

"Sure," I said, following her down the hall. Lots of people figure I know all about electricity and electrical appliances because I read meters. The truth is if my toaster breaks down, I either take it to a repair shop or buy a new one. I usually tell people that, but I didn't feel like telling it to her at that particular moment. The way she was dressed, I would have followed her anywhere and looked at anything she wanted to show me. I sure enjoyed looking at the way her ass moved inside those panties.

"In here," she said, leading me into her bedroom.

"OK," I said. "What is it you want me to look at?"

"This," she said with a flourish, reaching behind her and unhooking the little red bra. It happened so fast that her tits were free and swinging before I even knew it. "And this," she added, stripping the panties down her legs and kicking them across the room. For one long instant, she stood there stark naked while I just gaped. Then she took a step toward me. "Come on," she said. "I know you don't have a lot of time. I want you to fuck me."

Quickly, she threw herself backwards on the bed, opening her legs to show me everything. I didn't need to be told twice. I unbuckled my belt and dropped my pants and shorts down to my ankles. My cock was already sticking straight out in front of me, hard as a rock.

She sat up halfway and reached out toward me. "Use this," she said, handing me a condom. Something about the fact that she had it ready and waiting for me turned me on even more. I rolled that thing onto my dick faster than ever before. I started unbuttoning my shirt, but the lady was impatient.

"Don't bother with that," she said. "Just fuck me. Now! Then read the meter and leave." She knew what she wanted, and I figured the least I could do was give it to her. Stepping out of my pants, I went to the bed and dropped down between her legs. I inched forward so that I could ease into her, but she didn't want to wait.

Roughly, she grabbed my cock and yanked on it, pulling me toward her. Then she steered it to her snatch and thrust it inside. All of a sudden, I felt the wet heat of her surrounding me. It felt like she had a fever of 110 degrees. I mean, her pussy was steaming.

She squeezed my cock with her vagina, using her muscles to clasp me tight. Then she started moving her hips up and down, running the clinging lips of her pussy both ways along the length of my hard-on. I was on top, but she was completely in control. She set the pace; she established the rhythm. For the first time in my life, I was fucking a woman who I couldn't keep up with.

While she bucked and heaved under me, she kept saying things like, "Oh, yes, fuck me, you big strong cockman. Shove your dick deep into me. Ram it in hard. Yes, like that. Like that." She was driving me crazy.

Her voice got louder and louder, until she started shouting, "Fuck, fuck, fuck, fuck, fuck," just like that. She rode so hard that I thought the bed was going to bust. Then, she busted. All her cries strangled in her throat as she started to come. It was all I could take. I started coming, too, pumping hard and shooting my load with all the strength of my nuts.

I don't think the whole thing took more than about two and a half minutes. As soon as we were both done coming, she laughed long and loud. "Oh, yeah," she hollered. "That was a good one. Now you better get the fuck out of here."

Pushing me off her, she rolled out from under me and walked toward the bathroom. "See you next month," she called. "Hey, and don't forget the meter."

I pulled on my pants in a hurry, ran down to the cellar, read the meter, and left. It wasn't until about fifteen minutes later, when I was driving to another location, that I realized I was still wearing the condom. One of the hazards of my job, I guess. I pulled it off and threw it out the window, laughing to myself as I thought about what had just taken place.

Now I count on my monthly fuck with Mrs. X, just as regular as clockwork. Only I bring my own condoms. It's the least I can do.

The trick is to try and get in and out, laid and all, in no more time than it usually takes to read a meter. She likes it that way. To tell the truth, I do, too. It makes it so I can get right back on the job.

Of course, I'm still always on the lookout for more skin, and there's usually something to see. That's why I love my work so much. Hey, you think I might turn into a workaholic?

OFFICE TEMP

Jenny is only nineteen, but claims to have had more sexual experience than most women twice her age. She is small and compact, standing just a little over five feet tall, with full breasts and a well-rounded bottom. Her thick chestnut hair is shoulder length and is probably the first thing anyone notices when looking at her. Her green feline eyes flash against a background of creamy white skin. Her easy smile is flirtatious and seductive.

I can't help it. I'm a seducer of men. It just comes natural to me. Find 'em, fuck 'em, forget 'em. What turns me on the most is grabbing a quick one at work. That's why I like being an office temp. It's the ultimate sexual challenge.

I'm in a job for only a few days—never more than a week. My mission is to score before I leave. I pick my victim, find the place, lure him to it, and fuck his brains out. Then I'm out of there.

I started in high school. The other girls wanted to be cheerleaders and maybe get a date with the quarterback. I set out to fuck the entire team. All the teams—baseball, football, basketball. Hell, I even did the debate team. The girls called me a nympho, but I didn't care. They weren't getting laid, and I was.

That's not all I got out of high school. I learned word processing and computer operation and all the other skills that got me into the work world while they were just moving on to college. They call college higher education; I call it advanced high school.

I've been steadily employed since the week after graduation, and I've been fucking on the job since day one. Sex in the workplace really turns me on. I could have had about a dozen permanent jobs, but I just love temping: no real responsibilities, no worries to take home at night, and best of all, a constantly changing pool of opportunities.

For me, work is a groovy erotic game. I come into a new job knowing that I'm only going to be there for a day or two. My first move is to scope out the workplace and find the right location. I do that even before I pick out the guy.

In fact, sometimes the only reason I choose a particular guy is because of the spot I've decided to use. Once, for example, I resolved to get laid in the executive men's room. Since only three men had the key—the president, the vice president, and the comptroller—I had to seduce one of them. That took two whole days.

Most of the time it doesn't take that long for me to score, though. My record is just under two hours. Once, I managed to fuck two different guys on a one-day job. The first one in the elevator before lunch, and the second in the mail room just before closing. I remember how scared he was. He kept saying he couldn't do it because somebody was going to walk in any minute, but I was merciless. I just laughed and told him that only meant we'd have to do it fast. I took off my underwear and lifted one foot onto a table, unzipped his fly, got his cock into me, and finished him off within three minutes. I don't even remember his name, if I ever knew it.

It would be really hard to pick out the experience that turned me on the most, but here's one I'll never forget. I was sent to an insurance company that needed an extra word processor for the day they audited their files. The place was crawling with good-looking young claims adjustors, so I knew I was going to like it.

Within an hour, I had decided on the file room. It wasn't much more than a huge closet filled with rows of four-drawer cabinets. Because of the audit, it was getting a lot of traffic, which was what I liked most about it. I discovered a little corner alcove behind the last row of files. The idea of doing it in there was really hot because people were passing in and out of the room all the time to get and return files. The alcove was relatively hidden. As long as no one was looking for names starting with the letters *v* through *z,* it would be fairly safe.

Next, I selected the victim. I had my eye on one particular guy. He had been looking me over ever since I got there, flashing me a bunch of phony self-assured smiles. I've met lots of men who come on that way. They flirt outrageously until I let them know that I might really be hot to trot. Then they get scared and start backing down.

My belief is that they just go through the flirting motions because they think they're supposed to. But they're all so afraid—of losing their jobs, or losing their girlfriends, or losing their prestige, or losing something they think of as their dignity—that they wouldn't go through with it in a million years. Of course, the fun part for me is to make them.

Well, this adjustor, his name was Mark, looked like one of those to me. He was in his middle twenties, with short, very neat, blond hair. Really looked like a man on the way up. When he was sure I would notice it, he checked me out thoroughly and obviously. I guess I picked him because of his cocky smile. I really love to shoot a guy down, and he looked like he would be a perfect target.

The next time I saw him looking in my direction, I dropped a pencil and bent down to pick it up, giving him a good view of my tits. Then, when I sat up straight again, I accidentally brushed my arm against my skirt, so that it rose up high enough to show him the crotch of my pantyhose. The bait was cast.

I looked him right in the eye as I pulled my skirt back into place, not exactly smiling come-hither, but not exactly chasing him away, either. I could see from his expression that he was hooked. As I knew he would, he soon strolled over to my desk and introduced himself. After some pointless chatter, he asked me to have lunch with him.

"I don't know about that," I answered sweetly, "but I do know that if you meet me in the file room five minutes from now, you won't care about lunch."

It took him by surprise. He was used to being the come-on person, and I had just snatched that role away from him. But, of course, he couldn't really be sure what I was getting at. I saw his mind working behind his eyes, searching for a clever answer that would leave all his options open. To keep him off balance, I grabbed my purse and left my desk before he had a chance to respond. "Five minutes," I repeated, and headed towards the women's lounge, just beyond the file room.

While I was in the bathroom, I removed my hose and stuffed them into my bag. The plan was for me to be waiting for him near that back row of files. If he did have the guts to come in, I would waste no time getting acquainted. I'd just offer him an instant fuck behind the cabinets.

I was pretty sure he'd be terrified and look for a way to get out of it. But I also know that there isn't a man alive who can resist the scent of easy pussy, no matter how risky it turns out to be. He'd hate himself for it, but he'd go back there with me. If we got caught, that would be the end of his job. Me, I'm only a temp. What the hell do I care?

He surprised me, though. First of all, he was already there when I got to the file room. In fact, he was waiting for me in the very place where I had planned to wait for him. Trying to regain my advantage, I threw my shoulders back and my chest out in front of me and walked directly to where he was standing. Sending a quick look around the room to be sure that we were alone, I took charge again. "Quick," I commanded, "jump back into that corner before anybody comes in."

I expected him to stammer and flounder around the way they usually do when a too-good-to-be-true fuck falls into their lap, but Mark wasn't like the other guys. Without a word, he stepped around the corner and crouched behind the files as if he had done it a million times before. I turned out to be the one who hesitated, but not for long. He reached out and grabbed my wrist, pulling me in after him.

I thought he might be bluffing and decided to put him to the real test. Reaching straight for his fly, I unzipped it. He surprised me again by pulling up my skirt and putting both hands on my bare ass. Instantly, his pants dropped to his ankles, and his stiff cock stuck out in front of him.

Just as he was lifting me up and pulling me onto his boner, I heard the sound of someone entering the room. Mark must have heard it, too, but it didn't stop him. His dick slid into me without any fumbling, just like it was driven by radar control. The possibility of getting caught wasn't bothering him a bit. He was more brazen than me. He was going to get laid, and nothing was going to interfere with that.

Swiftly and soundlessly, he began fucking me. Long, persistent strokes that drove the tip of his cock hard against my cervix and then pulled it almost to the outer limits of my pussy. I wrapped my legs around his thighs, using the muscles of my ass to slam myself furiously against his rocking pelvis.

I heard the door open again, and another person entered, making two people in the room besides us. We could hear them talking with each other, exchanging light banter as they searched for files. One said something about the Williams file, and I knew that meant he would be coming near our little alcove. Mark grinned. He knew it, too. It didn't seem to worry him at all, though. If anything, his gyrations became more violent. His cock drove deeper and harder into my pussy. Maybe the idea of getting caught was as much of a turn-on for him as it was for me.

I felt him swelling inside me, and I knew that meant he was going to come. I was going to come with him. I bit hard on my lip to keep myself from crying out. I wondered whether he would be able to control his own sounds. Just as the orgasm began, I heard a drawer opening in the file cabinet we were leaning against, and I knew that somebody was less than two feet away, oblivious to the fucking going on under his very nose.

Mark shot his load in silence, drenching me with semen, but never even breathing hard. We kept rocking and rolling until the others had left the room and we were alone again. As I uncoiled my legs and straightened my skirt, he buckled his belt and said, "Not bad. Not bad." Those were the only words spoken during the entire episode.

I found it hard to concentrate after that, but somehow I managed to return to my desk, put on the dictation headset, and get back to work. For me, sitting at a desk and typing after fucking one of my fellow employees is half the fun of sex in the workplace. An hour later, totally lost in my work, I was startled by a light tap on my shoulder. I pulled off the headset and spun my chair around.

Mark was standing there with a foxy smile on his face. "There's a door just to the right of the elevator," he said. "Go to it in ten minutes and walk inside. I'll be waiting."

I didn't work at all after that, just kept my eye on the clock. I was enjoying this weird role reversal and wondering what my male counterpart had in mind. When the time came, I walked toward the elevator, trying to look as though I had some business purpose. Without glancing around, I went through the door as he had instructed.

I found myself in a dark little area behind a movie screen. It sounded like a training film was being projected onto the other side of the screen, with a group of new employees watching it. Nothing was between them and me but the thin material of the screen. I didn't move, for fear that they would hear me if the voices on the film suddenly went silent.

I stood there in total confusion, until I suddenly felt fingers stroking their way up my thigh. Mark was lying on the floor right next to where I was standing, feeling me up inside my skirt. I couldn't see him, but there was no mistaking his touch or his insane boldness.

He tugged at my hem, letting me know he wanted me to lie down with him. I did. When I reached for him in the dark, I realized he was naked. He had been waiting for me that way, certain that I would join him. With efficient movements of his fingers, he worked at my buttons and snaps until all my clothing was piled beside me and I was as naked as he. Rolling me onto my back, he mounted me and shoved his cock into my waiting pussy with one quick plunge.

He fucked me with wild abandon, without giving a shit about who might hear or discover us. I rocked with him and rolled with him, letting each masculine thrust press me flat against the floor and then hanging on to him with my arms and legs as he rose for another thrust. Within seconds, we were exploding into orgasm.

That time, Mark didn't bother to stifle the sound. His hoarse breathing seemed to fill the room and his guttural grunts seemed to echo off the walls. Encouraged by his cries, I added my own to the erotic clamor. Nobody came to investigate, but I can't believe they didn't hear us.

The moment our climax was finished, he pushed my clothes into my hands and began getting himself dressed while I did the same. We made it with only a fraction of a second to spare. Just as we were going through the door, I heard a voice on the other side of the room say, "OK, that's it. Somebody take down the screen."

I've worked in lots of offices since then, but I haven't met anyone as bold or as exciting as Mark. Sometimes, I play with the idea of maybe going back and seeing him again, but I'm afraid that would spoil it. I mean, the whole fun of the thing was the spontaneity. Looking for him wouldn't be very spontaneous, so I'll just keep temping and watching for new opportunities.

7

GROUP GROPE

WHEN WE WROTE *WHISPERED SECRETS*, WE INTERVIEWED
hundreds of people about their sexual fantasies. It did not surprise us
to learn that group sex was one of the most popular. It seemed that,
from time to time, almost everybody imagined having sexual contact
with multiple partners.

In the 1970s, the subject drew a great deal of media attention. Almost every American city had a suburb that was reputed to be an or-
giastic hotbed of swinging and swapping. Most serious researchers have
concluded that the phenomenon probably took place less in the parlors of middle-class America than in the imaginations of sensationalis-
tic journalists and their readers.

Group sex has haunted human imagination for thousands of years.
The walls of ancient Indian temples abound with bas-relief sculptures
showing large groups of people coupling in positions designed to bring
each reveler into simultaneous contact with as many others as possible.
So many sex scenes depicting threesomes, foursomes, and moresomes
have been found on ancient Greek and Roman pottery that some ar-
chaeologists are convinced the activity was common in those societies.

Among the people who talked to us about their sex lives, group sex
was far from common. Most had enjoyed it in their fantasies and ex-

pressed curiosity about it, but not many had ever indulged that curiosity. We did find a few who said they described actual group experiences, and because the group sex fantasy is almost universal, we have included two of their stories.

Each story demonstrates a different attitude. The woman known as Sunshine says that having sex with her three partners turned them into "one loving organism." To Stu and his wife, Sheila, sexual contact with the strangers they met at a club had no spiritual significance; it was something they did to give a lift to a marriage that had started feeling stale.

KINDRED SPIRITS

The woman who told us this story is a librarian and looks like she is trying very hard to fit the dowdy conservative stereotype of her profession. She is in her late forties, but appears considerably older. Her drab grey dress is buttoned and belted, doing nothing one way or the other for her medium frame and slightly overweight figure. Her hair, also grey, is pulled severely back into a bun. Her face is without makeup, the only hint of color coming from delicate pale blue eyes, framed by steel-rimmed glasses. We were quite surprised when she asked us to refer to her as Sunshine, which she says is her old hippie name.

Don't let my appearance fool you. I'm a very sensuous and passionate person. My husband, Irwin, and I have an extremely satisfying sex life. Maybe my background has something to do with that. I wasn't always the frumpy middle-aged librarian you see before you. Back in the early sixties, I was a genuine flower child, part of a hippie tribal family. We called ourselves the Spirit Group.

There were about twenty of us Spirits. We lived together in upstate New York on a beautiful piece of land that belonged to the family of one of our members. We turned it into a real commune. We grew a lot of our own food and even kept a cow for milk and cheese. Occasionally, some of us would get jobs in the neighborhood, and it was understood that when we did, we would turn our earnings over to the group. There were a few old cabins on the land, but we all lived in a big barn that we separated into a kitchen and a huge living area.

Irwin knows about the Spirit Group, but he has no idea of the sexual things we did. I have no intention of telling him, either. But I do know this—when Irwin and I have our best sex, it's because I'm thinking about those communal days. That's what turns me on the most.

We Spirits believed in freedom of all kinds. Most of all, we believed in sexual freedom. We thought of ourselves as one big happy family, and we thought that a commitment to one exclusive partner would interfere with that feeling. So one of our unwritten rules was that pairing off was a no-no. We talked about love a lot, but it was always communal love. We regarded sex as love's perfect expression.

Life was easy and uncomplicated, then. When the weather was warm, most of us went naked. It felt free and right. We tried to avoid game playing and manipulation, which we called "ego tripping." When someone wanted to have sex, he or she was just supposed to ask, "Do you want to play?" The idea was that we were so comfortable with each other that you could say no without anyone feeling hurt or rejected. It just meant that you weren't into it at the moment.

At one time or another, every one of us had some kind of sexual contact with every other one of us. Sometimes, when we wanted privacy, we did it in the woods or in one of the cabins. But most of the time, we had sex wherever and whenever the mood struck us. It didn't matter if there were others around. If they were busy doing something else, they might ignore us. If they wanted to, they might watch, or they might even join in.

To me, the best times were when all of us got it on in the living room of the big barn. Sometimes, these group sessions would go on for days at a time, with everybody tripping on LSD or mescaline. They were like Roman orgies, but we didn't think of them that way. To us, they were expressions of group love.

We would change partners indiscriminately, sometimes hardly aware of who we were with at the moment. Of course, those were the days before AIDS. Women might have sex with other women. Men might have sex with other men. Three or four or five people might have sex with each other, all at the same time. It didn't matter. We were like one loving organism.

Of course, in spite of our credo, we all had our favorite sex partners and our favorite people. The Spirits with whom I felt the closest were a woman named Glow and two men named Sergeant and Spock. Lots of times, the four of us would sleep together on a huge pile of pine needles under the stars. If one of us woke up, he or she would turn to whoever was nearby and begin stroking and touching. Pretty soon, all four of us would be making love and rolling around together in the softness of our forest bed. We thought that, by having sex together, we were merging our souls to become one person. We truly loved our communal life and family.

Obviously, our existence was too idyllic to last forever. I guess the same can be said about the whole hippie movement. Around 1969 or 1970 the "Manson Family" murders became news, and suddenly, everyone everywhere was against hippies and communes. People in the surrounding area started giving us a hard time. Eventually, the people who owned the land we were living on told us we had to leave.

Our group broke up, and little by little, the Spirits all went their separate ways. A few have become very successful business people—millionaires. I can't help thinking that the time we all spent together contributed to their success in some way.

Everybody stayed in touch for a while, but eventually, I lost contact with most of the Spirits, except for Glow, Sergeant, and Spock. The four of us have remained good friends. We write to each other regularly and talk on the phone fairly often.

Sergeant is an insurance broker, happily married for more than twenty years. Spock, who works on a commercial fishing boat, has never married. He's had lots of relationships with women, but none has ever lasted more than a few years. After two divorces, Glow gave up on marriage and raised five children on her own, while carving out a successful career as an author. She says that Spirit Group life helped her become a writer by teaching her how to express herself freely and without inhibition.

The four of us have made it a tradition to get together once a year for a weekend reunion. Irwin has never objected. He assumes that all we're doing is talking about old times. What he doesn't know, and what I don't intend to ever tell him, is that we do more than talk. We actually relive our communal experiences. Doing so makes me feel young and free again. I don't want to sound like I'm rationalizing, but in a way, I think it actually revitalizes my marriage.

For years, we had our reunions at a hotel or resort in some central location, but ever since Glow's kids grew up and moved out on their own, we've been meeting at her house. She's got a great place in the country, with plenty of peace and quiet and solitude. There are lots of trees, and I guess it reminds us all of the Spirit Group commune. The last time we got together there was just about a year ago.

When I arrived, Glow came to the door and threw her arms around me. She was totally nude. As the two of us stepped inside, I saw that Spock and Sergeant were already there. They, too, were naked. While Glow and I embraced, the guys began tugging at my clothes, unbuttoning and unsnapping me until I wasn't wearing any more than they were. Everybody started hugging everybody else and soon we were all rolling around on the floor, just like in the old days.

I could feel hands moving over me, fondling my bare breasts and buttocks. I didn't know whose hands they were, but it didn't matter. I closed my eyes and surrendered to the comfort and security of being with my old family again.

"We've been at it for a while," Spock whispered. "You've got some catching up to do."

I let my three beloved friends arrange my position on the floor. First, they moved my arms away from my body. I could feel fingers and lips caressing my hands and trailing up to my shoulders. Someone nuzzled my armpit. Then, I felt them tugging gently at my ankles.

Abandoning myself completely to their will, I let them move my legs apart. Just a little at first, and then wider and wider. I kept my eyes tightly closed as they exposed me to their communal gaze. I was already excited beyond belief. I loved the idea that they could all look at me and see anything they wanted. I knew there were three pairs of eyes on me. Then I felt their touch.

Six hands moved across my skin—thirty individual fingers caressing me. I could feel each and every one. Three pairs of lips. Three tongues. Glow's nipples grazed the soles of my feet. The tip of someone's penis stroked the palm of one of my hands. I just lay back and let it happen, floating on the dreamy billows of delight. I felt safe and secure and loved.

Warm lips closed over one of my nipples, and I didn't even try to guess whose they were. A moment later, another mouth began sucking at the other nipple. I could feel hot breath on my vagina and knew that a third mouth was about to touch me there. It didn't matter whose mouth was where. All that mattered were the wonderful sensations that flowed through my body. I knew that my three friends wanted to express their love for me by making me feel as good as they possibly could. Nothing was beyond them. None of my desires would be left unfulfilled.

A tongue slipped between my labia, making me draw my knees back automatically, to spread my legs wider. Fingers opened my vulva, and I knew that one of my partners was holding me open for another.

I didn't know who was who, but I was distinctly aware of three different mouths taking turns on my genitals, each with a slightly different technique. When someone kissed me on the mouth, I could taste the musky fragrance of sex on his or her lips. Maybe it was my sex, maybe someone else's.

I felt a penis nudging gently at my lips and opened my mouth to take it in. I began to perform fellatio, trying to give back some of what I was receiving. The other penis was sliding into my vagina, entering me gently and lovingly, letting my vulva become accustomed to its thickness before it plunged deep inside. It began stroking slowly in and out. I felt it growing thicker and longer with each thrust, until it swelled so big it seemed to fill my very being.

Hands stroked and petted my breasts, rolling my erect nipples to bring me to even higher levels of rapture. The room around me was gone. I was no longer stretched out on a carpeted floor. I was lying on a bed of pine needles, merging with my three kindred Spirits in the same old way. I felt young again, and free. The hands and lips and genitals of my loving friends were carrying me back across the years, helping to recapture my youth.

I opened my eyes so I could bask in the heated glow of their blissful faces. Spock was on his knees beside me, his sex sliding in and out of my mouth. When I stroked it with my tongue, he smiled adoringly and took my face in his work-worn, but tender, hands.

Glow was seated next to me, squeezing and kneading my breasts and watching intently as I devoured Spock's thrusting penis. Her fingertips touched lightly at my swollen nipples, sending torrents of elation throughout my body. Leaning forward, she dabbed at the point of each nipple with the very tip of her tongue.

Sergeant was buried deep within me, filling my vagina with his heavy thickness. He was on his knees, moving his hips forward and back to drive himself further inside. Every instroke brought me to the brink of a scream, and every outstroke made me fear that he would withdraw completely. When it seemed that his penis was about to plop out of me, I tightened the muscles of my vulva, trying to hold on to him as long as I could. Then he reversed direction, searching again for my core with the tip of his organ.

I felt an orgasm building and did nothing to hold it back. That was the best part of these sexual reunions. We were going to have sex all weekend long. There was no limit to the number of orgasms we would share. There was no reason to exercise any control whatsoever. We were totally free, devoted to nothing else but the pleasures of making love.

I felt Spock's penis thickening and I knew that his climax was also approaching. Suddenly, he pulled out of my mouth. His cries announced his orgasm as he spurted jets of hot fluid onto my breasts. Glow's hands rubbed his semen all over me.

"Yes," I crooned, my voice amplified by indescribable surges of ecstasy. "I'm going to come. Oh, yes, make me come. Oh, I love you all.

Oh, I love you." And with that I just let go, the shocks of sexual climax making me twitch and writhe uncontrollably.

I could feel Sergeant rearing back as his own orgasm burst upon him. His penis pulsed as it shot his seed deep into my waiting channel. My eyes closed again. I abandoned all consciousness and gave myself over to the wonderful sensations.

When I drifted back to reality, I saw Glow on her hands and knees with Sergeant behind her, his tongue lapping at her sex. Spock was on his back beneath her, sucking on her nipples. His penis was hard again, standing straight up like a post with its base anchored in the damp dark thatch of his pubic hair. Languidly, I reached out and took his erection in my hand. Gently, barely making contact, I stroked it slowly up and down.

The pace continued for the entire weekend. We made love in every possible position and in every conceivable combination. The only things I enjoyed more than my own orgasms were the ones I gave my friends and the ones they gave each other. For a short time, we relived our old unselfish communal love.

At night, we all slept together on the living room floor, just like the old days under the stars. We rarely slept more than an hour at a time, though, because when ever any one of us woke up, the mutual loving started all over again. No one seemed to mind being awakened by an exploring hand or tongue.

By the time the weekend was over, I was physically and mentally exhausted. I felt so satisfied that I was sure I would never need sex again. All through the long drive home, I thought about the things we did and the fun we had. It had a strange effect on me.

The closer I got to home, the less tired I felt. Not only that, but my sexual appetite returned. When I arrived, I was filled with energy and so turned on that I positively jumped on Irwin and dragged him into our bedroom. We made love for hours before I even had a chance to say hello.

It happens like that whenever I go away for a reunion with my kindred Spirits. Irwin doesn't seem to wonder why. He probably figures it's the separation that makes me so hungry for him. He's glad that at our age we can still have passionate and explosive sex.

I'm glad, too. I honestly believe that's a benefit of my connection with the Spirit Group. As long as I live, whenever I feel the need for a sexual spark, I will have only to think of my Spirited friends to get myself all turned on. Come to think of it, it's getting to be reunion time again.

ORGY CLUB

Stu, forty-three, works as a foreman for a manufacturing company. He is about six feet tall, but his lean frame makes him appear taller. His light brown hair is neatly cropped, giving him a conservative look. Something about the cunning glint in his almost-black eyes hints that there might be a savage hiding inside his middle-American exterior. Stu says he and his wife recently discovered a new sexual turn-on.

I guess we needed something different. Sheila and I have been married for the past twenty years. So long that sometimes we think like one person, even though we look as different as two people can possibly be.

Sheila's short, only about 5′1″, and a little overweight. But I like her like that—nice and fleshy. Her eyes are light grey. Her hair is on the long side and bleached blond, but not that brassy kind of blond. Even at forty, she's still a knockout. I think so, anyway.

Things have usually been good for us, but you know how it is. Everything gets stale after a while. For the past few years, I had felt that our sex life wasn't as exciting as it ought to be. I could see that Sheila thought so, too. Maybe that's why I perked up my ears when I heard Dennis shooting off his mouth in the lunchroom down at the plant.

He was saying something about an orgy club where people meet for free sex. Snickering like a high school kid, he said the phone number was 555-FUCK. Dennis is about the most unadventurous guy you'll ever meet, and everybody knows he's never done anything in his life, so nobody was really paying attention to what he was saying. For some reason I did, though.

I was sure he was talking through his hat, but just for the hell of it, I dialed the number as soon as I got back to my office. I guess I was expecting some kind of X-rated recording. I was rather surprised when a businesslike male voice answered, "Forest Club."

Startled, I stammered something like, "Uh, can you tell me something about your operation?"

"Certainly," he said. "The Forest Club is a nonprofit association devoted to the study of sexual freedom. We have meetings every Saturday night from nine P.M. until everybody goes home. Dues are thirty-five dollars per couple per meeting. We supply snacks, but if you want something to drink, you've got to bring your own. If you'd like to attend, just drop in."

I don't really know what I was thinking, but I scribbled down the address and directions he gave me, still not knowing for sure what the Forest Club was all about. When I got home from work that night, I told Sheila about it over dinner. She was just as intrigued as me.

We were both kind of mystified about the description the guy on the phone gave me. That thing about a nonprofit association devoted to study sounded like some stuffy group of professors sitting around and reading papers to each other, but the sexual freedom part fascinated us. There seemed to be a hidden message in the dues being figured per couple and per meeting. Also, the part about meetings starting at nine P.M. on Saturday nights and lasting until everybody goes home didn't sound much like an academic symposium. Maybe it really was an orgy club like Dennis said.

Sheila got a dreamy look and murmured, "I'd love to watch people doing it, in the flesh. If we went there, do you think we might get to see something like that?"

I was certainly interested, but I really hadn't expected her to feel the same way. I shouldn't have been surprised. I told you we think alike. "What the hell," I said. "Why don't we go find out. We can use fake names, so nobody will ever know who we are. If it turns out to be talk, talk, talk, we can always leave. If it is some kind of sex club, we can watch as long as they let us. If they kick us out, what have we got to lose? Thirty-five bucks?"

* * *

I'll admit we were both kind of nervous that Saturday night when we arrived at the driveway of the Forest Club. It looked like a big old private house with a parking lot behind it. When we pulled in, right about nine o'clock, there were lots of cars parked there. So far, we still couldn't tell what we were in for. When we walked in the door, I had that butterflies-in-the-stomach feeling.

There was an old guy sitting on a high stool just inside the doorway. When he said, "Good evening," I thought I recognized his voice as that of the guy I spoke to on the phone. He asked for our dues, and as I reached for my wallet, I looked past him into the living room of the house. It seemed like an ordinary cocktail party. There were couples sitting around on couches and chairs with drinks in their hands having casual conversations.

When I gave the guy our money, he said that the hostess would show us around. Right on cue, a woman stepped out of the hallway and greeted us. She was wearing a tight low-cut dress that had a classy look to it but left no doubt that this wasn't no seminar, baby.

Leading us into the living room, she pointed out the direction of the bathroom and kitchen and told us to make ourselves comfortable. In the kitchen, there was a long table covered with food and surrounded by people eating off paper plates. They seemed to be making normal conversation.

She pointed to the hot tub room down the hall and said, "The best way to enjoy the Forest Club is to go exploring. You can look into the private cubicles all you want, but if there's anyone in them, you shouldn't enter without being invited. It's different in the group room. There, anything goes, as long as nobody objects. It's your club. Make yourself at home." We had no questions, so she left us on our own.

I thought it would help Sheila relax if we sat for a while in the living room before checking the place out. I got to admit I kind of needed relaxing myself. The hostess hadn't gotten explicit, but there was an awful lot of suggestion in what she had said. I really felt nervous. Glancing around the room, I found us an empty love seat, and we settled into it.

A few people were standing around with paper plates or drinks in their hands. Most of the ones sitting down were fooling around. One couple was locked in a hot passionate kiss. We could see his hands traveling all over her body. The girl didn't seem to mind it any. In fact, her hands were fiddling around in his lap.

On the other side of the room, a woman was leaning way back on a couch with her eyes closed. Her blouse was completely unbuttoned, and her boyfriend had his hands inside her bra. I felt myself getting excited.

At first, we were embarrassed about looking at the things going on around us, but no one seemed to mind, or to notice us, for that matter. In a soft voice, Sheila said, "If this is what goes on in the living room, I wonder what the people are doing in those other rooms she told us about."

"OK," I said, still feeling a little jittery. "Let's go have a look."

Even though we were kind of prepared for it, the hot tub room was a bit of a surprise. There were two big redwood tubs in it, and they were both filled with naked people. Some were touching each other, but most were just sitting in the bubbling water and talking to each other. There were chairs around the tubs, and we decided they must be for observation, so we sat down for a while.

In one of the tubs, a big woman with huge tits was sort of bouncing up and down in the water. I couldn't help staring at those boobs as they bobbed and swung from side to side. Suddenly, I realized that I was being kind of obvious about it, and I got embarrassed. I stole a quick look at her face, hoping she hadn't noticed. Boy, was I surprised when she smiled and winked at me. I wondered if Sheila had seen it.

I would have liked to just sit there and watch the naked women, but after a while we started to feel awkward. We were completely dressed and maybe we looked like a couple of perverts or Peeping Toms. So, trying to be inconspicuous, we quietly got up and left to continue our explorations.

Just down the hall was a little room with its door standing open. There was nobody inside, so we felt pretty bold about going in. It was weird.

There were all these devices that I thought existed only in sex movies. Hanging from the middle of the ceiling was a black nylon harness that a person could sit in and swing on. The bottom was all open, so maybe someone else would get underneath. I don't exactly know how it was supposed to be used, but my head was filled with lots of ideas.

One wall was almost completely covered with mirrors. On the floor in front of it was this long leather cushiony cylinder. Sticking right up from the center was a thick leather dildo. I could imagine a woman fucking herself with the false cock while riding the cushion like a horse.

"I don't believe this stuff," Sheila gasped. "Do you think anyone actually uses it?"

As if in answer, a couple entered the room at that very moment. The man was wearing nothing but a towel wrapped around his waist. The woman was dressed in a bra and panties, but she stripped them off as soon as she got into the room. She climbed into the swing and spread her legs wide to wrap them around her partner's waist. He dropped the towel and hunched forward. I was too embarrassed to look straight at them, but I could see his cock aiming at her opening.

Taking my hand, Sheila whispered, "Let's go."

When we stepped into the hall outside, we both giggled. "Wow," I said. "Maybe we should have stayed. That would have been something to see. But I guess we'd better be careful until we understand the etiquette of this place."

"From the looks of things," Sheila said, "I think we'll find plenty to see. The hostess said we could look all we want into the cubicles. Which way do you think they are?"

Heading in a new direction, we walked on further until we came across a large bedroom, dimly lit. We heard voices coming from all over the room. Well, not exactly voices. More like moans and groans of lust. Sheer curtains divided the room into five small compartments. The floor of each compartment was covered by a large mattress. The curtains created a feeling of separateness, but really didn't give anyone privacy, because you could see right through them.

We stood in front of the first cubicle, speechless at what we saw. A man and a woman were on the mattress, both nude and sixty-nining like mad. He was on his back with his feet pointed towards us. She was straddling him, with her crotch right over his face and her head between his legs. We couldn't exactly see what they were doing, but it was obvious.

Sheila and I have watched porno movies together, but this was the first time we ever saw anything like that in person. We were both shaking with excitement. We stood there in silence for a long time, just fixed on the scene unfolding before us. We had been told it was all right to watch, but I don't think we would have been this comfortable about it if they had been able to see us. As it was, they were both so busy eating each other out that they probably didn't even know we were there.

After a while, our curiosity made us move on. There was a deep purring moan coming from the next mattress, and we were drawn to it. By then, we had become bold enough to stand right in front of the curtain so that we could have a really good view.

There was a woman lying face up on the mattress with her legs spread far apart. Her pussy was wide open, and I could look right into it. There were two women kneeling at her sides, stroking her body with their hands. When they both began playing with her nipples at the same time, I heard Sheila gasp. This made the woman look up at us, and I want to tell you that was weird. Here she was with two other women all over her tits, and at the same time, she was looking right into my eyes and smiling.

I felt a little ashamed about the way I was staring and thought it was time to move on. I sort of nudged Sheila, but her feet were fastened to the floor. She was entranced by the erotic sight. The woman on the mattress whispered hoarsely, "It's OK. We don't mind if you watch. Do you want to come in?" We just shook our heads and stood there, numbly staring at them as they went back into action.

Then we heard grunts coming from the next compartment and found ourselves moving unconsciously toward it. There was a man lying on his back and a woman riding him like a bucking bronco, humping her hips up and down as she drove him in and out of her. They must have just started coming because they were shouting together in a kind of orgasmic chorus. We watched until she fell forward, spent, and they both stopped moving.

Sheila was squeezing my hand in a way that told me that she was getting as turned on as me. My cock was so hard it looked like I was carrying around a spear in the front of my pants. When we shuffled into the hallway, I tried to hide it by walking behind Sheila and pressing myself against her fleshy ass.

We heard lots of voices and sounds coming from another room and knew that it must be the group room. I was feeling kind of breathless with excitement. Neither of us could quite believe that a place like this existed, or that we had found it.

It must have been the largest room in the house. The entire floor was covered with foam rubber about four inches thick. There was a pile of shoes next to the doorway under a sign that said, "BAREFOOT, PLEASE." Adding our own shoes to the pile, we slipped in quietly.

My eyes were immediately drawn to two couples screwing loudly in a far corner. The women were lying on their backs, side by side, while their partners fucked them in the missionary position. After about ten strokes or so, the men quickly withdrew and changed places. I stared, fascinated, as they slid into their new partners. The women were moaning and groaning, and I wondered whether they were as aroused as me by the idea that each time the men stuck it to them, they were still wet from their other partners. After a few strokes, they changed partners again, and again.

I could have stood there watching them all night, but there were other sights to attract my attention. Like the threesome—one guy and two girls—tied up in a daisy chain. They were lying on their sides in a circle, each going down on another. I was especially turned on by the sight of one woman licking another woman.

I glanced at Sheila to see whether she saw what I saw, but she was looking at a different part of the room, where another threesome was at work. A red-haired woman was on her hands and knees getting fucked from behind by one guy while she was sucking on another guy lying on his back in front of her. Her head was moving up and down in rhythm to the strokes of the guy who was in her pussy.

Sheila gravitated towards them, taking me with her. After being at the Forest Club for less than an hour, we were watching others have sex without feeling embarrassed about our fascination. We got close enough to see every detail. I watched the action, forgetting about my own wife for a minute. Suddenly, to my surprise, Sheila dropped to her knees and reached for the naked woman's dangling tits. I couldn't believe what I was seeing. I wanted to grab her and drag her out of there before she got into trouble. But, I've got to admit, I also wanted to see that other woman's tits in her hands.

Sheila touched them lightly, stroking downward towards the nipples. My cock was drooling at the sight. The woman lifted her head for a moment, letting the guy's hard-on slip out of her mouth. She looked at Sheila and smiled. Then, with a sigh of ecstasy, she went back to the blow job.

Sheila was totally into it now, squeezing and kneading the woman's big swinging tits. I never saw anything so exciting in my life. Without even thinking about it, I got down on the mattress next to her and began stroking the naked woman's legs and ass. In a muffled voice, the redhead said, "Oh, yeah, smack my ass. Smack it hard."

So I obliged her. Just as the guy behind her drew back for his thrust, I whacked her naked backside, bringing a roar of excitement from her throat. Without waiting for an invitation, I did it again, the sharp noise of the slap echoing in the room.

Suddenly I felt Sheila's arms around me, and we rolled onto the mattress together. The air around us was filled with sounds of passion. We were surrounded by it. We were high on it. We were totally absorbed in it. I'm telling you, it's like we were consumed by a desire that was stronger than anything either of us had ever felt before.

As we kissed and embraced, we began tearing each other's clothes off, very much aware that we were exposing each other to a dozen pairs of eyes. I know it was making me hotter that all the women could look at my cock if they wanted. The men could look at Sheila, too, but that didn't bother me at all. The sex hunger was in control.

I kissed my wife's lips and then moved my mouth over her naked chest to suck at her nipples. She was moaning louder than I had ever heard her moan in our bedroom. I dipped my face lower, trailing my tongue over her belly until my mouth was buried in her slit. I let my excitement take over and became oblivious to everything else. From the way Sheila was bucking and rolling against me, I knew she was in seventh heaven.

I wanted to see her face, but when I looked up at her, I got the shock of my life. The two guys who had been doing the redhead were now doing Sheila. They were kneeling beside her, feeling up her tits. I felt an instant pang of jealousy, but I also found it very exciting. As I listened to my wife's pleasure sounds, I imagined how good it must feel for her. I kind of wanted to stop them, but also I kind of didn't.

Before I could make up my mind what to do, I felt the light touch of the red-haired woman's fingers on my back, stroking downward over my ass. Suddenly, I didn't feel any reason to stop Sheila from having her fun. In fact, I wanted it to be wonderful for her. I went back to licking her, giving her everything I knew she liked.

For a while the woman's hands explored my body the way the men were exploring Sheila's. She stroked my cheeks and the back of my scrotum. Then she started rubbing my cock up and down. It felt so good, I can't begin to tell you. I felt like I was going to come. Somehow, that seemed like something I should only do with Sheila, so I shook off the redhead, climbed up onto my wife, and slid inside.

The other three fell back to watch Sheila and me finish what all of us had started. I pounded in and out of her until the climax came to both of us together. We let ourselves go, not caring about how loud we were getting. Matter of fact, we were probably trying to attract as much attention as possible. It felt like dynamite.

At some point, I think everybody in the room must have been watching. But when our orgasm was done, they all went back to their own little games. While they were busy with one another, Sheila and I put our clothes on and left the room, the party, and the house.

We were quiet for a while as we got into the car and drove away, probably a little ashamed and not quite sure of what to say to each other. I just couldn't stop thinking about what took place. Sheila had to be thinking about it, too. As soon as we got home, we ran into the bedroom and had some of the hottest sex I could remember.

We have talked about it a lot since then. Usually, it turns us both on real fast, and we end up having a hot old time. We haven't had a chance to get back to the Forest Club yet, but every time we want a lift, we talk about what happened there that night. We're going to go back real soon.

8

SEX FOR PAY

PROSTITUTION HAS BEEN CALLED THE WORLD'S OLDEST PRO-
fession. Certainly, it has an ancient history. In Old Testament times,
Babylonian women were expected to sacrifice their virginity to the gods
by having sexual intercourse with the first man who placed a coin in
the temple collection basket. This practice, known as cult prostitution,
was forbidden to the Israelites. Sex for pay, in general, was not. Genesis tells the story of Judah, one of Abraham's great-grandchildren, and
his daughter-in-law, Tamar. After Tamar accepted payment of one goat
for having sex with him, Judah declared her to be a righteous woman.

In most of the United States, prostitution is illegal, but its illegality
has not eliminated the practice of buying and selling sex. Some argue
that prostitution will always exist because it fills a need for people who
have no other sexual outlet. The descriptions we received from people
we interviewed make it clear, however, that sex for pay may involve a
special excitement that goes far beyond the satisfaction of biological
needs.

Attitudes of the people we interviewed varied so greatly that, to present a balanced picture, we have included four of their stories in this
chapter. All describe sex for pay as a favorite turn-on, but each gives a
different reason. The similarities and differences in their points of view
furnish an interesting counterpoint.

Although both of the women in the following stories associate prostitution with power, Lynee says it's because she is paying and Nancy because she is being paid. Nancy regards the money that changes hands as a reflection of her personal worth. Lynee sees it as something that gives her the right to demand sexual fulfillment.

The men also express different perceptions about the role that exchanging currency for sex plays in their arousal. Larry visualizes the Nevada brothel he visited as an erotic supermarket, focusing on the availability and the variety of sex offered. The cash in his pocket was significant only because it made his purchases possible. Walt's relationships provide him with convenient sexual outlets. For him, sex with prostitutes is a "spice." Although the intercourse for which he pays lasts only a minute or two, thinking of sex as a business transaction is what turns him on for months at a time.

PRIVATE DANCER

Lynee says that she not only came from money, but married money as well, and her appearance backs up her claim. Her fashionably short, fashionably frosted hair is done twice a week at a chic salon with a recognizable name. The color of her nails, like the frames of her glasses, always matches her outfit. The money she spends on her appearance makes her look younger than her fifty-five years. She says she was brought up to believe that her only work should be finding and maintaining a wealthy husband. When she and her husband divorced, it was understood that she should not have to change her affluent lifestyle.

Hamilton had fallen in love with a younger woman, and the guilt was more than he could bear. So, as always, he used money to try and gain spiritual absolution. His request for a divorce did not bother me as much as either of us expected it to. I almost felt relieved. I had never really been happy with him. When Hamilton moved out, I wasn't even lonely. He had never been home much, anyway.

As far as I was concerned, our sex life was always abysmal because of my total lack of power. Everything was the way Hamilton wanted, no matter how I felt. I never found intercourse satisfying, and Hamilton knew it, but didn't care. When I tried asking him for other things, he ignored me completely. At such times, he would just mount me and have his pleasure, almost as if he were trying to show me that he was in charge.

I gave up on sexual satisfaction rather early in our marriage. When he wanted to have intercourse, I serviced him. It wasn't often, and it never took long. My own needs drove me to masturbate, which gave me temporary relief from my mounting frustrations, but never really turned me on. I stopped expecting anything more.

I continued masturbating after the divorce, and it continued to relieve my tensions, but I did it without strong feeling. It was like brushing my teeth—it needed to be done, but there wasn't anything exciting about it. Sex just was not a turn-on. I even stopped thinking about it.

Then, one afternoon at lunch, a dear old friend asked how I was surviving the divorce and handling the sexual emptiness. That was when I finally recognized what a sexual vacuum my whole life had been. Bitterly, I said, "I'm used to it. I'm in my fifties and I've never had good sex. Never once have I had an orgasm with a partner. If I haven't had it by now, I never will. So, I guess I'm doing all right."

My friend smiled knowingly. "It's too bad women like us don't talk about that sort of thing more often," she said. "I came to the same conclusion after my divorce. I'll bet most of our friends have, too."

"So, what do we do?" I asked plaintively. "Just give up forever?"

"That's not what I did," she said, lowering her voice to almost a whisper. "I called for a private dancer."

Something about the phrase sounded illicit but exciting. I was intrigued. "What exactly is a private dancer?" I asked, feeling that I, too, should lower my voice.

"Oh, my dear," she said. "You're going to love this. It's a man who comes when you call him and does anything you tell him to do—sexually." I was agog. "When I got divorced, a friend told me about them, just as I'm telling you," she continued. "She gave me a number to call and told me to say I needed a private dancer for an audience of one. A few hours later, I felt like a new woman. Now, I call them regularly. I have a feeling you will, too, once you give them a try.

"They provide the most gorgeous young men. Each one they send is more beautiful than the last. Most of them are aspiring young actors, with bodies like Greek gods. They're all experts at pleasing a woman sexually. I just tell them what I want, and they do it. We've got the money, and they've got the talent. The more we pay them, the better they are."

I couldn't believe what I was hearing. She might be calling them private dancers, but male prostitutes is what they were. Shocking as it was, the idea of paying to have my sexual needs fulfilled interested and even excited me. It was a way to be in charge. My money would give me the upper hand.

My friend didn't wait for me to ask. She wrote the name and phone number of the agency down on the back of a card and handed it to me. "If you do call them," she said, "you're the only one that will ever know. I won't even ask you about it. I urge you to give it a try."

That afternoon, I moved about in a daze of excitement. I thought about all the sex acts I had wanted Hamilton to perform, and I imagined ordering an attractive young private dancer to perform them. I had never felt so turned on before. When I masturbated later that night, it was with actual pleasure, accompanied by my powerful new fantasy. I was certain, of course, that a fantasy was all it would ever be.

The following day, the fantasy about buying sex continued to turn me on. And the day after that. The idea kept growing inside my imagination until it became an absolute obsession. By the time two weeks had gone by, I decided I would call the number.

Even after I made the decision, though, it was a few days before I actually built up the nerve to go ahead with it. The combination of nervous trepidation and excitement made my hands shake as I punched the agency's number into the phone. My throat was dry. When a woman's voice answered with the company name, all that came out of my mouth was a croak. But when she said, "Can I help you?" I reminded myself that I was about to place an order for service, something I knew very well how to do.

"Yes," I said. "I'm interested in a private dancer . . . for an audience of one." When the words came out, my burst of confidence began to fade. I was nervous again, half expecting that the world would end, or worse, that the woman on the phone would mock me.

But without missing a beat, she replied in a surprisingly mercantile tone, "We have three dancers available this afternoon. Do you have any preferences?"

"Good-looking?" I said timidly. "And obliging?"

"All our gentlemen meet that description," she said. "I'll send Victor. I'm sure you'll be pleased with him."

She explained the agency's fees and promised that Victor would arrive within an hour. Every word frightened me and turned me on a little more. I gave her my address and hung up, trembling with anticipation.

All right, I had placed my order. But a stranger was on his way to my home to have sex with me. I considered calling back to cancel. In an effort to stop myself from doing so, I reminded myself repeatedly that I was a customer, and that a customer has power. I looked out the window, half expecting to see a naked man stepping out of a cab at that very moment. Instead, I blinked at the bright afternoon sunshine. It was comforting in a way. It seemed safer, somehow, to do this during the day than at night.

My feelings swung back and forth like the pendulum of a clock. Mostly, I was scared. But each time I reminded myself that he would be my employee—someone that I had hired and therefore had a right to control—I found my fear giving way to arousal. Then I would think about the reality of being naked with him, of being touched by him, and my fear would return.

I don't know how I survived the wait or how many times I decided to call back and cancel the order, but I managed to get through it. When the doorbell rang, I was still nervous, but glowing with anticipation. I felt like a young girl facing a new and exciting adventure of sexual discovery.

When I opened the door for him, Victor turned out to be even more handsome than my friend's description had prepared me for. He was positively stunning, with jet black hair and big brown eyes. He was tall and muscular and moved with the grace of a cat. His sensuous fluidity was so sexy that it got me thinking about the reason for his presence, and I found my knees getting weak. My confidence had fled. I didn't know what to do or say.

He knew how to ease my embarrassment. "What a lovely lady," he murmured, taking my hand in his and pressing it to his lips. "This is my lucky day. Shall we step inside?" He invited me into my own home, and I followed dumbly behind him.

We sat on the couch for a moment and made idle conversation, like two people meeting in a dentist's waiting room. Then, without further preamble, he said, "Tell me, my dear. What kind of sex do you like?" I couldn't think of any way to make words come. After a moment's silence, he added, "And I'll have to collect in advance."

Miraculously, that calmed my nerves and turned me on again. I was the purchaser, and he was the merchandise. I was buying him. When I reached for my purse and handed him the cash, I was taking control of a sexual situation for the first time ever. As he took the money from my hand, I felt a tremendous rush of excitement. I knew exactly what I wanted, and I had just paid for the right to demand it.

"I want oral sex," I told him. "I want to feel your mouth on me. But not in here. Come with me into my bedroom." Obediently, he followed.

I hoped for an opportunity to watch him undress, so I sat on the bed and waited to see what he would do. Then, with a flush of excitement, I remembered that I was the boss. "Take your clothes off, please," I commanded quietly. I had never been so turned on in my life.

He obeyed at once, casually tossing his garments one at a time onto my vanity bench. His chest was broad and powerful. His thighs were thick and muscular. When, at last, he stripped away his black Jockey shorts, I saw his huge organ bob into view. He was genuinely excited— that's something a man can't fake.

I stood up, letting my hands drop to my sides. "Now undress me," I ordered. Hamilton had never undressed me, not once during the entire course of our marriage. Not even on our wedding night. I never had the power to ask him. But when I gave Victor the order, his duty was to obey.

He stepped toward me and began to undo my buttons. His strong hands moved slowly, gradually removing my clothing and exposing my body. All my anxiety was gone by then. I felt nothing but arousal.

His fingertips brushed at my bare skin, fanning embers of desire that had been dormant for years. I had never been totally naked in front of any man except Hamilton, and the way he looked at my body had always made me feel vulnerable. But standing nude in front of Victor gave me a sense of power. As soon as he removed the last garment, he fell to his knees before me and wrapped his arms worshipfully around my hips. I felt his hands caressing my buttocks as he buried his face in my mound.

"Oooh," he sighed, "you are a beautiful woman." His words excited and comforted me at the same time. "Please," he whispered, "let me make love to you."

"Yes," I answered. "I want you to make love to me. I want you to make me come." I had never said anything like that before. Just speaking so explicitly was a turn-on.

He pushed me gently toward the bed, moving forward on his knees. When the backs of my legs touched the mattress, I eased myself down until I was lying on the bed with my feet still on the floor. His catlike body moved between my knees until I felt the heat of his breath on my inner thighs and the hungry yearning place between my legs.

Then he kissed me, his mouth and lips all over my tender secret parts, where no one had ever kissed me before. Victor moaned as he nibbled and caressed my quivering tissues.

I was swimming in a heated pool of ecstasy, unfamiliar sensations whirling throughout my body and soul. I had never felt such splendor. I had never been treated so lovingly. His lips and mouth danced over my swollen labia, opening me, exploring me. Then his tongue slipped inside. I moaned in an agony of newly discovered pleasure.

Victor's hands ambled over my nudity, stroking and caressing my hips and abdomen until my breasts cried out for comfort. Unhurriedly, he found his way there, his fingers tracing spirals over the globes of my breasts and then gently rolling my erect nipples. His tongue moved in and out of me, emulating the rhythm of intercourse, but bringing me sensations that intercourse never had. Instinctively, I wrapped my legs around his back, trying to pull him tighter against me, trying to bury his tongue even deeper inside. He swept it up and down the length of my opening, sending waves of pleasure through my entire being.

Then he began concentrating on the tense little button at the top. I had long ago learned to give myself pleasure by touching that sensitive spot, but it was nothing like the heat intensifying with every flick of his talented tongue.

I had bought this, and I felt entitled to maximum pleasure. "Oh yes," I ordered. "Lick me right there." The novelty of giving sexual commands magnified my excitement. He didn't need to be told what to do, but I needed to tell him. "Oh, yes. More . . . more of that. Suck me. Lick me."

I was astonished by my obscene demands. But it felt so good—not just the wonderful sexual sensations, but the extraordinary feeling of being in charge. "Give me more of your tongue," I commanded. I was awkward at first, experimenting with my new sexual power. His instant obedience increased my sense of authority, and I became bolder. "More of it. Yes, lick me there, and there. Softer now. Still softer. Yes, lick it like that."

I was drunk with power. Every time I told Victor what I wanted, he did it. And everything he did brought me closer and closer to completion. I was torn between the desire for completion and the longing to make the experience last forever. Then I realized there was no reason to hold out any longer. If I wanted another orgasm, I could buy it.

"Keep licking me," I said. "I'm going to come in your mouth." Like a gushing torrent, I burst forth, flying over the cataract of climax as his hungry lips and tongue brought me to orgasm. I made sounds that my bedroom walls had never heard before. I enjoyed making them, and I even enjoyed hearing them. My orgasm lasted forever. It was the first time in my life that someone else had given me that precious gift.

His mouth stayed in contact with my sex until long after my spasms had subsided. Then, gently, he disengaged himself and got off the floor to lie beside me on the bed. He held me in his arms with my face pressed against his bare chest, allowing me to rest in the security of his embrace. I felt myself absorbing his sexual confidence. "Thank you," I murmured. He said nothing. He understood.

I continued to lie naked on the bed after he was gone. I was more relaxed than I had ever felt before and truly satisfied for the very first time. I understood, at last, what money could accomplish. My sexual hunger would never again go unsatisfied.

Every time I call the agency, I have them send a different private dancer. So far, I've always had them make oral love to me. Maybe soon I'll try intercourse. I don't call every time I feel a sexual urge. That would be too self-indulgent, and unnecessary, since I'm enjoying masturbation a lot more than I ever did before. Now, when I'm stroking myself, I think about my private dancers and my newfound sexual power.

BROTHEL

Larry, twenty-two, is a computer technician. His light brown hair is tousled and begs for a comb. He is thin and angular, appearing even taller than his six feet. The black frames of his thick eyeglasses give his hazel eyes a scholarly look. At first, he is shy about discussing his sexual experiences, but as he warms to the subject, his freckled face takes on an expression of boyish excitement.

My sex life is pretty slow at the moment. Actually, you might say it's at a standstill. I don't have a steady girlfriend, and I don't really go out much. I do a lot of jerking off, but right now, that's about the extent of it. I like to fantasize when I'm doing myself. I really only have one experience worth fantasizing about, but that one ought to be enough for anybody. It turns me on every time I think about it. Without a doubt, it's the most exciting sexual thing I ever did. It happened just about a year ago.

* * *

I was turning twenty-one and thought I ought to celebrate. I was work-ing for a software company, and I had a week's vacation coming, but I didn't have anyone to celebrate with. So I decided to go to Reno, Nevada, alone. I had heard it was a really hot town. I guess I was think-ing about the things I could do there at twenty-one. I mean, I could drink. I could gamble. I had heard there were whorehouses nearby, too. I guess I thought it would be a fitting way to come of age.

Actually, it wasn't all that great. Drinking isn't much fun if you're drinking alone, and I didn't really enjoy the gambling. I inquired about the whorehouses, but they were real expensive. I just couldn't afford to pay a hundred bucks to get laid, no matter how horny I might be.

I went to a couple of ass-and-tits shows, but even that got old after a while. I'd just sit there by myself, nursing a six-dollar bottle of beer, watching the half-nude girls pretend to dance, while my pecker strained against my pants so hard that it hurt. Then I'd go back to my room and jerk off again. But I never really was satisfied.

I was thinking of going home early, when the thunderbolt struck. I went to one of those buffets where you get all you can eat for about five and a half dollars. As usual, there was a long line of people waiting to be seated. As the line moved slowly forward, I found myself standing in front of a dollar slot machine. More out of boredom than anything else, I put a dollar in the slot and pulled the handle. And bingo, I hit the jackpot. Lights started flashing, bells started ringing, and a small crowd gathered around me. "Four thunderbolts," someone shouted. "Hey, this guy just won twenty-five hundred dollars."

At first, I couldn't believe he was talking about me. But sure enough, a casino lady in one of those short-skirt outfits came over with a key to turn off the bells and whistles. "Congratulations," she said. "You're a big winner."

I was in a daze when I went to the cashier's window for my payoff. I couldn't tell you what we said to each other. I just remember taking a fistful of bills and stuffing them into my pocket and then running to my room.

For a while, I just sat there, counting the money over and over again. After a while, it made me feel kind of sad. Here I had received a fabulous windfall, enough money to do just about anything, yet I couldn't think of a thing to do with it. Then I remembered the whorehouses and my mood started to brighten. I could certainly afford to go to one of them after winning a jackpot. I flipped open the yellow pages, but I couldn't find any listings. I tried "prostitutes," "brothels," even "entertainment." But nothing.

I had seen some flyers in the street with pictures of nearly naked women, so I ran outside and grabbed one from a newspaper dispenser. It was full of ads for whorehouses. I took it back to my room and called a few of them, but they wouldn't give me any information over the phone.

One of the ads in the flyer was for a taxi service that said it specialized in transportation to the brothels. So I called them up and told them to meet me in front of the hotel. A few minutes later, I was on my way.

The cabbie recommended one particular place, so I let him take me there. It was way outside of town—in another county, I think. The trip took over half an hour. I was still in a daze and I don't remember much about the ride, except worrying about getting ripped off and wishing I had left some of the money in the hotel safe.

When the cab pulled up in front of the place, I started to get nervous. It was a big metal building, like a giant warehouse, with a lot of trailers attached. It looked kind of industrial. Not at all what I pictured a brothel to be. By then, it was pretty late and starting to get dark. I was thinking of asking the cabbie to wait for me, but he said not to worry, that the brothel would call for a cab to bring me back to town whenever I was ready. I paid the driver and got out.

Nervously, I opened the front door of the warehouse. Stepping inside, I found myself in a kind of a cage, with a steel mesh door in front of me and a thick black curtain on the other side of it. There was a little window with bars, like a teller's window in a bank. A woman on the other side of the bars said, "Yes, can I help you?"

I guess I stammered a bit, before saying, "Well, I saw your ad in one of those papers. Can I come inside?" I heard a little click and the wire mesh door popped open. "Have a nice time," she said, without cracking a smile.

When I shouldered my way through the black curtain, it was like stepping into another universe. I'll never forget it. There was a huge smoky room, filled with people and the sounds of conversation. There were quite a few men, but more women. Couches and chairs were everywhere. Some of the women were sitting in them, while others walked around. I couldn't believe what I saw. Some of the women wore sheer sexy nightgowns, with their nipples showing through the material. Others wore ordinary blue jeans and cowboy shirts, all buttoned up to the neck. I remember one sitting on a sofa in a red sequined gown, which was hiked up so far that I could see the crotch of her black panties. A few were walking around in underwear—just in a bra and panties. I think one was wearing a garter belt.

The women were all different shapes and sizes: some short and petite, some fat and fleshy. One looked like a child, with her hair in pigtails and little girl clothes. Another was about seven feet tall, with shoulders like Hulk Hogan. There were white ones and black ones and some that looked Asian. There were dozens of Hispanics. One girl looked like an Indian. She was even dressed like one, with a fringed buckskin outfit and a beaded headband. There was something for everybody.

I just stood there staring all around me and feeling my cock getting hard inside my pants. I hadn't ever seen so many different women all in one place at one time. The part that turned me on the most was knowing they were all there to fuck. I knew I could have my pick of any one of them. It was like being in an erotic supermarket with shelves full of every imaginable delicacy and delight. I was blinking my eyes in wonder when a woman came up to me and said, "Hi, honey. Want a date?"

She was in her late thirties, I guess, and kind of overweight. She had olive-colored skin and dyed-black hair. She wore only a pair of black fishnet stockings and a red bra and panties. The panties were real brief, and I could see little curls of black hair poking out from the leg bands. The bra was also brief, and her huge tits were flowing out of it. I wanted to reach out and touch one, but I had the feeling that wasn't the way things were done around here.

She wasn't the best looking woman in the room, and I probably wouldn't have picked her if I had more time to think things over. But I was so hot and horny by then that all I could think of was getting a piece of ass. Also, I was real nervous. "Uh, how does this work?" I asked. "How much do—"

"Let's not talk about that here," she interrupted. "Come with me to my room. I'll give you a real good time."

There were doors all over the place, but she knew exactly where she was going. As she walked, I watched her big round ass moving in front of me. The little red panties formed a tiny triangle that barely covered the crack, and her cheeks rolled from one side to the other as she moved. Working up my courage, I patted her lightly on the ass as I came up behind her.

"Oh, yeah," she said softly. "I'm going to give you a real good time."

We walked down a labyrinth of corridors until she stopped in front of a closed door. "This is my room," she said, opening it and stepping inside.

The room was tiny, hardly bigger than the bed that was in it. Putting her fingertips on my chest, she pushed lightly until I was sitting on the edge of the mattress. "Do you like my titties?" she asked, pulling the bra cups down to show me two big melons with big brown nipples. She gave them a shake and laughed. "Go ahead and touch them," she offered. "I'm going to give you a real good fuck. Just one hundred dollars."

I cupped her boobs in my hands and said, "Sounds fair to me."

She stepped toward me, grabbing the back of my head and pressing my face between her tits. They were so big and soft that for a moment I thought I might just come in my pants.

"You got to pay first," she said, reaching down to unsnap the front of her bra at the same time. A moment later, she had stripped off the brief little panties and was standing naked, except for the fishnets. Her belly was flabby and sort of pouched down to hide a little bit of her pubic hair, but at that point it didn't matter to me. I handed her a hundred dollar bill and stood up to start tearing my clothes off.

As soon as I was naked, with my cock sticking straight out in front of me, she wrapped her arms around me and we both fell onto the bed. I buried my face in her bosom again as we rolled around on her mattress. The feel of her naked belly against mine and of her legs wrapping around me made it hard for me to breathe. She rolled onto her back and pulled me on top of her. Instantly, she reached down and took hold of my cock, bringing it to her waiting pussy and swallowing me up inside of her.

She was all soft and wet, like she was just made for sex. As soon as I got it in, she started moaning and shouting, "Ohh, yeah, baby. Ohh, you got such a big cock. Oh, yeah, fuck me baby. Oh, yeah, fuck me." The next thing I knew, I was shooting my load inside of her, pumping it out like there was never going to be an end.

Before I knew what hit me, she was up and slipping her panties back on. I just lay there watching her and thinking that it was over before it even began. As she put her bra on, she said, "Got to go now, baby. Unless you want to fuck me again. This time, I'll do it for seventy-five."

That was when it really hit me. I was in a sexual warehouse. I could get laid as many times as I wanted, with as many different women as I wanted. "No," I said. "I think I'm going to look for someone else."

"I got just the girl for you," she said. "When we go back into the parlor, I'll introduce you to Dolly."

"Maybe later," I answered, feeling more self-assured, even a little bit cocky. "I'll look around on my own for a while."

"Sure," she said. "You have yourself a real good time. That's what we're all here for. And if you want me again, I'll be around. I give a real good blow job, too."

Her words planted the idea in my head. Next time, I was going to get some of that. I followed her back into the parlor—what a funny name for it—and looked around again. That time, I didn't wait for a woman to come up to me. I picked out a good one. She was wearing a transparent nightie. I could feel my cock getting hard again already.

The girl I selected was slight, with slim hips and small titties. Her nipples were small too, but a wonderful bubblegum pink. The hair on her head was blond, but the patch of pussy hair that showed through her nightgown was a rich dark brown.

I walked right up to where she was sitting alone on a love seat and said, "Hi. What's your name?" She patted the cushion beside her, and as I sat down, she said, "I'm Bambi. Are you enjoying yourself tonight?"

"Yes," I said. "I just finished with one of your girlfriends, and now I'm ready for you." I'm not usually comfortable talking to girls, but I had started to feel like a big shot, a high roller. "Which way to your room?"

"I like a man who knows what he wants," she said with a chuckle. "I'll bet you even know what you want me to do."

"Exactly," I answered, "but I'll tell you about it when we get there."

I followed her through the corridors again, walking past door after door until she opened one of them and we went in. The room was just like the other one—all bed and nothing else. Without waiting to be told, I handed her a one hundred dollar bill and said, "Take off the nightgown. I want to see what you look like with nothing on."

Without a word, she pulled it over her head, exposing her naked body to me. Her skin was milky white, without any trace of suntan. She must have spent all her time indoors, fucking one man after another. The idea excited me in a kinky kind of way. Her pert pink nipples were the same color as her mouth and the same color as her pouting pussy lips, which I could see poking out from the jungle of her bush.

She expertly undressed me, tossing my clothes onto the floor. "Nice tool," she said, stroking my cock with her hand. "Now what was it you wanted me to do?"

"Give me a blow job," I said. I don't think I ever spoke with such confidence and authority in my life.

"Good choice," she said, "I can't wait to get that sweet cock of yours in my mouth." She sank to her knees in front of me, her face within inches of my bobbing hard-on. Sticking her tongue way out, she licked the head with a slow circular motion that made it even harder.

"You like that?" she murmured, cupping my balls in her hand as she slid her tongue up and down my shaft. "And that?"

"Yeah," I grunted. "I like it a lot." I knew I'd be able to hold out longer this time because I had shot a load only a few minutes ago. Bending slightly forward, I reached down and fondled her tits, taking the erect little nipples in my fingers and rolling them back and forth.

"That's nice," she said. As she licked me, her fingers began sliding up and down my inner thighs, caressing my flesh and working their way up towards my asshole. No girl had ever touched me like that before. I wanted it to go on forever.

"Let's move to the bed," I said. "I want to put my finger in your pussy."

Quickly, she got on the bed and lay down with her legs spread wide. I lay beside her, facing toward her feet so that I could look at her pussy while she sucked on me. As I felt her mouth nibbling at my hard-on again, I started running my fingers through the dark curls of her pubic hair. The smell of sex seemed to fill the room. I was sure it was coming from her pussy, and I tried to imagine how many different men she fucked every day. I slipped a finger in and found it juicy and warm.

Then her mouth completely engulfed my cock, sending hot shocks of pleasure through me. The combination was incredible—her lips and tongue working my dick, my finger sliding in and out of her pussy, and the spicy scent of sex filling my nostrils. Even though she was a professional, I'm sure she was as turned on as I was. She was moaning and groaning all over the place.

Her humming moans were vibrating wildly around my cock. I knew another orgasm was coming. The best part was that I could pump it right down her throat without even asking. My cock was swelling and rearing up like a stallion, the hot stuff in my balls working its way up through my pipes. When the first spasm struck me, I hollered "Oh, yeah, I'm coming." She kept sucking and swallowing, her tongue working up and down the underside of my prick to bring more and more stuff out of it. She acted like she was enjoying it, her mouth milking me the whole time.

I had my finger rammed deep into her snatch and was twisting it around and around in rhythm to the pumping of my orgasm. When I looked, I could see a foamy white liquid coating my knuckles and lubricating my thrusts. I liked seeing her so juicy.

Finally, when I was totally spent, she let my dick slip out of her mouth. Before I knew it, she was out of the bed and putting her nightgown on again. "Time to go, sweetie," she said. "Unless you want me to do you again. Only seventy-five for the second go around."

"No," I said, completely sure of myself. "I like a little variety."

"I can introduce you to my girlfriend," she said. I was beginning to realize that this was the standard sales pitch around here.

"Thanks," I answered. "But half the fun is shopping around."

"I understand," she said, handing me my clothes as an obvious hint that I should hurry up.

A minute later, I was back in the parlor. This time I decided to slow down a little. So I got a Pepsi from a machine in the corner and sat in one of the chairs, sipping it while I looked around. Every once in a while, one of the girls would approach me and we'd chat for a while. But when they saw that I wasn't quite ready to buy, they'd drift away and leave me by myself.

After maybe an hour, one particular girl caught my eye. She was tall and lean with shiny black skin and sultry brown velvet eyes. Really beautiful, with tits and ass in perfect proportion to the rest of her body. I had never been with a black woman before and decided that she would be my next partner.

She was wearing a simple white minidress that accentuated the long graceful curves of her legs. Every time she moved, I could see muscles rippling in her shapely thighs. I really wanted her. When I got up from the chair, I was surprised to realize that I was hard again. Under normal circumstances, I probably would have sat down and crossed my legs to hide the bulge, but this was a sex shop. No reason to be embarrassed here.

I walked over to the goddess and said, "Hi. I've been watching you."

"Have you now?" she answered, smirking erotically. "And what did you have in mind?"

"Lots of things," I said. I felt like bragging a little. "I've already had two of the women here, but I have a feeling you're going to make it a grand finale. Do you have any suggestions?"

"Mmmm," she said softly. "If you want something really grand, how about making it a threesome. I know just the girl. We'll even do each other a little while you watch."

I felt my cock twitching and chills racing up and down the back of my neck. I had always imagined being with two girls at once, even the part about seeing them do things to each other. In this sexual wonderland, I didn't have to content myself with just imagining it. It was waiting for me on a silver platter. All I had to do was buy it.

"It'll cost a little extra," she said, "but I promise we'll be worth it."

She beckoned to a Hispanic woman standing nearby, who came over to join us. Her face looked exotic and mysterious, her almond-shaped eyes flashing with fire. She was fleshy enough to be sexy, but not an ounce overweight. She had on a pair of tight jeans and a red halter-top that showed her big tits and outlined a thick pair of nipples.

The three of us went through a door that led to one of the trailers attached to the outside of the building. It was bigger than either of the two rooms had been, with a king-sized bed. As soon as we got in, the black one told me the price was three hundred dollars. I paid it without a whimper.

The girls immediately began undressing each other, their fingers lingering over each other's soft flesh as they removed the garments from one another's body. I stood watching as they fell naked to the bed and began sucking and licking each other's nipples. I couldn't tear my eyes from the sight.

The black girl had nipples the color of bitter chocolate, and they crinkled and tightened as the other one's pink tongue slid over them. Her pussy was shaved. The charcoal color of her outer lips contrasted with the rose-colored interior. It was the first time I had ever seen a black woman's pussy and also my first time to see a shaved one. The combination was very erotic.

I saw the Hispanic woman's fingers toying with the shiny black labia and slowly slipping in between them to begin thrusting in and out. She got to her hands and knees and bent over her friend, showing me her naked ass while she began licking the hairless black slit. Little by little the two women moved until the Hispanic's knees were straddling the head of the black woman, who craned her neck so that she could lick some pussy, too.

I stood there staring as they sixty-nined. I could see each woman's tongue driving deep into the other's snatch. Without taking my eyes off them for a second, I took off all my clothes and joined them on the bed.

I stayed on my knees alongside them. The black girl's back was to the mattress, and she was writhing and wriggling as she buried her face in the other woman's juicy crotch. The Hispanic was still on her hands and knees, her ass held high in the air as she was licked from beneath, her back sloping forward so she could suck the black girl's pussy.

Then the black woman's hand reached out for me, feeling for my cock and pulling on it to draw me into the action. I crept up to the Hispanic's swaying ass, letting my stiff dick brush against it as I moved into position. I kneed my way forward, feeling a gentle hand aim me into the waiting wetness of the hot slit.

As I hunched my pelvis to bury myself in pussy, I opened my eyes wide to take in the scene. The Hispanic was on all fours humping her ass back against my belly as she went down on her partner. The other girl was lying on her back, her face only an inch from the tight combination of my cock and the Spanish woman's pussy. I could feel her hot breath on my balls, and then her tongue, as she licked me and her friend at the same time.

As turned on as I was, I was able to hold back pretty good because I had already gotten off twice that night. I just kept driving in and out and experiencing the dream of having two women at once. After a while we changed positions, so that I was fucking the black one while the Hispanic girl licked my nipples. Then I lay flat on my back while they gave me a double header blow job.

I can't count how many different positions we played with. I can't even remember them all. I know I got my three hundred dollars' worth with those two girls. When I came at last, it was the best orgasm I have ever had.

Of course, you know what happened then. The girls hurried back into their clothing and offered me another ride for only two hundred dollars. By then, I was completely shot. There was nothing left for me to do but leave with a head full of memories.

Back in Reno, I ended up losing the rest of my winnings, but I went home a happy man, with a vacation to remember. I know it was a once-in-a-lifetime experience. Without a doubt, it was the greatest turn-on of my life.

Now, when I'm in bed alone getting myself off, I think about my night at the Nevada brothel. Inside my head, I bring myself back to that sexual supermarket, where there was no limit to the erotic possibilities. I close my eyes and I think of all the women I had and all the women I could have had, and that takes me straight to heaven.

ESCORT

Nancy, thirty-four, is tall and thin, with big round eyes that are almost as dark as her long black hair. Her face and figure are attractive, but she wears a perpetually cynical expression with the barest hint of a smile, suggesting that she carries a secret deep inside her.

My husband is a cheap son of a bitch. Maybe I ought to thank him for that, because it led me to the only thing that has ever really turned me on.

When I was growing up, life wasn't all that good. My family didn't have any money, and I never got anything I wanted. Everyone I knew had a lot more than me. When I met Doug, I thought all that was going to change.

I had a lousy retail job, and Doug was one of the store honchos—the controller. None of the salespeople really knew him, but they all talked about him as if they did. They used to say he knew how to turn a dime into a dollar. Now, I know how he does it. By squeezing. Nobody can squeeze more out of a dime than Doug can.

I was only twenty-four then and very naive. He was fourteen years older than I. When he asked me out, he might as well have been Prince Charming showing me that glass slipper. I couldn't believe his royal highness would possibly be interested in one of the commoners.

The first few times he took me out, I was impressed. It didn't take all that much to impress me in those days. As far as I knew, the height of class was any restaurant with tablecloths. I decided to get him to marry me. I wasn't really in love with Doug, but I liked him well enough. He obviously made plenty of money. I was full of ideas about how that would change my lifestyle. Lifestyle, hell, I thought he was going to change my life.

I had gone out with a couple of guys, but never anything serious. I guess I had done as much fooling around in the back seat as any other girl in my set, but somehow I managed to hang on to my virginity. Maybe I was saving it for a dowry. I don't know. Anyhow, I thought I might be able to trade it for a wedding ring.

It worked. The first time I went to bed with Doug, I bled and I cried. It made him feel guilty. I don't think he had ever been with a virgin before. When I started to blubber about how I always wanted to save it for my husband, he got real tender. The next day, he asked me to marry him.

During the first couple of years, I felt affluent. I was living better than I ever had before. Instead of a cheap apartment, like I was used to, we lived in our own home. Our furniture was solid, not the kind of junk I had grown up with. Best of all, I didn't have to work. I started making a better class of friends, mostly the wives of men that Doug associated with.

Soon, I began to notice that my new friends lived a whole lot better than I did. They ate most of their meals out, for example, while Doug still expected me to cook for him every night. They bought their clothes in fancy little boutiques, while I was still getting mine at chain stores in the mall.

That was when I first realized how cheap Doug is. I went to one of those boutiques and picked out an outfit I really liked, but when I asked Doug for the money to buy it, he turned me down flat. He started bitching and moaning about how he wasn't made of money. When I told him I was tired of wearing the same kind of stuff I wore when I worked as a salesclerk, he said I wasn't being creative enough. He even suggested that I ought to start looking around at garage sales and swap meets. Imagine that!

I thought sex might be the way to change his mind. After all, it was how I got him in the first place. Up to that point, our sex life had been kind of colorless. Doug was more interested in making money than he was in having a good time. Sex was not high on his agenda. I was usually the one who initiated it. I didn't have much experience, but I had a good imagination. There were some things I had always wanted to try and I figured the perfect time was at hand.

So that night in bed, I used my mouth on him. It was the first time for me. To tell you the truth, I think I enjoyed it more than he did. After I sucked on him for a few minutes, he insisted on screwing me. The minute he got inside, he came. That was all right with me. At that point in my life, I had never had an orgasm, anyway, so I didn't know what I was missing. But it didn't make any difference about the outfit. When I asked him again the following morning, he just said no. And he repeated the suggestion about shopping at garage sales. I tried a few more times to win him over with sex, but it never got me anywhere.

After a while, I just gave up. That's how it was for a couple of years. I was still on Doug's strict budget, and I was still wearing inexpensive clothing. As far as sex was concerned, there didn't seem to be much point in it. About once a month, Doug would jab his hard-on against me under the covers, and I'd roll over and spread my legs for him. There wasn't anything in it for me and not much for him, either. I was so filled with resentment that I usually stayed dry inside for as long as it took him to finish.

*   *   *

I guess I would have gone on that way forever if it hadn't been for a phone conversation I had with Anita one night. Doug was working late, as usual, and I was bored, so I called her up. Anita and I grew up on the same street and have been friends, off and on, ever since we were kids.

She lived pretty good, and I always figured it was on the alimony she received from her ex. So while we were talking, I asked how he was doing. She said, "I have no idea. I haven't heard from the bum in years."

"What about the alimony?" I asked.

She just laughed. "Alimony? You gotta be kidding. I never got a dime out of him."

I was so surprised to hear it that I didn't think about manners. I just said bluntly, "Well, I know you don't have a job. What are you living on?"

Anita was silent for a minute. Then she cleared her throat. "I'm going to tell you something," she said, "but it's just between us. I do have a job. It's the best job I ever had. I'm a professional escort."

"What's that?" I asked. "What does that mean?" Somehow, I knew before she answered, but I needed to have it spelled out before I could be sure. She confirmed my suspicions.

"It means I fuck for money," she said. "A couple of times a week, a car picks me up and takes me to a nice hotel. The driver tells me what room I'm supposed to go to and waits for me in the car. I go in and meet some guy who gives me two or three hundred dollars to have sex with him. Sometimes even more than that. Then the limo driver takes me home. Not too shabby for a couple of hours' work, if you can call it work. I've got plenty of money, and I'm having the time of my life."

I was shocked, but the idea of having all that money interested me. I was fascinated by the sex part, too. To a girl who had never had an orgasm, sex was still a shining mystery. I asked a million and one questions, each answer making me think of more things I just had to know.

After a while, Anita said, "Sounds like you like the idea. Maybe you ought to try it yourself. You have the looks and body for it. I bet you'd make plenty."

I just sighed. "I wish I had the guts," I said. "It sure would be nice to have my own money."

For the next few weeks, I couldn't get the idea out of my head. One night I thought about it in bed and found myself becoming aroused. I reached out for Doug, but he just said he was too tired and went back to sleep.

Then one evening, I had a surprise phone call from Anita. She came right to the point. "I hurt my back this morning," she said, "and I can hardly move. But the escort service just called me with a job. I know the guy. He's real nice and a great tipper. How'd you like to go in my place?"

I didn't even think before I said, "I'll do it." Just like that. One minute I was a disillusioned housewife and the next minute I was a professional escort—a call girl!

The idea of going to bed with a stranger and getting paid for it was so exciting that I trembled all over. I rushed into the shower, and at Anita's suggestion, I put on my sexiest underwear. It wasn't silk like I have now, but it was lacy and revealing, and it was the best I could do. I had just finished dressing when I saw a white car stop in front of the house. I rushed out and got in.

The driver was a nice young fellow who seemed to know that I was new at this. When he pulled up at the hotel, he promised that he would be waiting for me right where he left me. He gave me the room number and told me to walk straight to the elevator without stopping to ask any questions.

I don't remember going through the hotel lobby, but I must have, because I do remember knocking on a hotel room door. It was immediately opened by a man who looked to be in his midfifties. He wasn't exactly handsome, but he seemed to have a nice gentle manner. He was wearing a satin robe embroidered with oriental figures. When he moved, I could see that he had nothing else on.

That was when it really hit me. He was going to hand me money and then I would be expected to do anything he wanted. I wasn't scared, I was excited. But I was also filled with anxiety because I was so inexperienced. All Doug had ever expected me to do was just lie there. I really didn't know how to do much more than that. Except for that one time, I had never even given a blow job.

Anita had told me I was supposed to collect three hundred dollars as soon as I got into the room. I thought it was going to be awkward, and I was relieved when he handed me three one hundred dollar bills right away. I was putting the money into my purse and trying to decide what to do next when he said, "Will you undress for me, please. Real slow." As he spoke, he sat down on the edge of the bed.

Suddenly, I felt sexy. Doug had never expressed a desire to watch me undress, but this man wanted to look at me. I loved the idea. I was probably clumsy, and I know I was inept, but I did my best. Slowly, I unbuttoned my dress and slipped it off my shoulders. I could feel his gaze devouring the swell of my tits inside my lacy bra. I'm not real big, but the look in his eyes made me feel like Dolly Parton. I started to reach behind to undo the snap and then I got an inspiration.

"I might need your help," I said. "Will you undo me?"

His breath got sort of wheezy as he reached up to oblige. When I realized that his hands were shaking, I gained a little confidence. He was as nervous as I was, maybe more so. That gave me the courage to roll my hips a little as I slowly lowered my panties. Even I found the sight exciting. My tits were like hard little cones, the nipples all wrinkled and puckered. My curly black bush was showing above the elastic of my panties. I could feel myself getting wet.

"I need your help with these, too," I said, as coyly as I could. "Will you pull them down for me?" I stepped closer to the bed and watched him reach out for my underwear. I felt the crotch sticking to my damp crack as he dragged them down my legs. Standing there naked and watching him drool with desire made me feel like a real woman for the first time in my life.

By the way he kept trying to swallow, I could tell he wanted to say something. I was beginning to realize that I was in the driver's seat. Finally, in a cracking begging voice, he said, "Would you please put one foot on the bed and let me look inside your pussy."

I felt a warm flood of arousal running over me as I obliged him. Stepping closer to where he was sitting, I placed my bare foot on the mattress beside him and held my crotch right in front of his face. I was close enough to feel his hot breath on my naked belly. He leaned forward, brushing his lips against my skin, and then his tongue was on me. Timidly at first and then a little more aggressively, he began to lick my pussy. He nibbled at the lips and kissed the tight little spot at the top of my slit. I had never before felt anything like it.

My sex felt like it was on fire. I was dripping wet. My juices were flowing over the pouting lips to fill his sucking mouth. Without even realizing it, I began bumping and grinding. His hands gripped my ass, pulling me tighter against him to drive his tongue inside me.

I began to groan and moan, making sounds I had never heard myself make before. One of his fingers burrowed between the cheeks of my ass as he tongued me. I wanted to scream and laugh and cry and thrash my fists all at the same time. Something unimaginable was building inside me, something I had never even dreamed about. And then, boom, it was there—the first orgasm of my life.

"Oh," I stammered. "I'm going to . . . I'm going to . . . " I knew I was going to have a climax, but I didn't know what to call it. Then it didn't matter anymore. I just exploded in his face, and he knew it. When I was done, I just stood there panting and trying to catch my breath.

"That never happened to me before," he said. "The other girls fake it, but this was the real thing. Wasn't it?"

"Oh, it was real, all right," I answered. "It never happened to me before, either." I'm sure he didn't have any idea how true that was. "You're really something. Now I'm going to take real good care of you."

Anita had told me he was a high tipper, and I'm sure that wasn't completely out of my mind, but I was feeling so grateful for what he had given me that I don't think money was my only motivation. I was finding out that sex could be everything I had once thought it was. I was seeing myself as a sexual being, someone who could give great pleasure to another person.

I operated on instinct alone when I got down on the floor between his knees and tugged his robe open. His cock was stiff and hard. To me, it looked positively huge. It filled me with wonder as I took it gently in my hands and began stroking it up and down.

He lay back and sighed, his body thrumming with desire. Each sweep of my fingers seemed to make his big dick get even bigger. I was enjoying the silky texture and the warm glow that came from his swollen erection. I could see a little drop of dew glistening at its tip. I had never seen that before, but then I had never really gotten a chance to look closely at a man's sex organ.

It excited me to think that I had power over him—the power to give him pleasure, the power of his desire. I licked that drop of moisture from the end of his cock, surprised by its salty sexy taste. Then, ever so slowly, I engulfed the head in my hot mouth.

I heard him groan and felt his body buck as I lowered my mouth to take more of him between my lips. I experimented with my tongue, looking for the places that produced the most dramatic reaction to my touch and finding them. I used my fingertips to stroke his balls while I licked up and down his rock-hard length.

I no longer felt inept. It seemed natural for me to please a man with my mouth and hands. I had come a long way since I got to that room. I went from novice to expert in less than seven inches. His rising excitement was my reinforcement. I knew from the sounds of his enjoyment that I had to be doing it right.

Suddenly, I knew things. I don't know how I knew them, but I knew them. I could tell by the way he seemed to rise and fall inside my mouth that he was nearing a climax. I was curious about how it would taste, how it would feel, when he pumped it down my throat.

But some instinct made me remember why I was there. I was a call girl, paid to please. Rubbing his cock with my hands, I lifted my head slightly and murmured, "What's your pleasure? Would you like to fuck me now, or do you want to come in my mouth?" I think saying those words and hearing myself say them gave me the biggest kick of the entire experience.

"Oh, yes," he hissed. "I want you to fuck me." As he spoke, he took my hands and eased me on top of him.

Believe it or not, I had never been in that position before. I guess Doug didn't like it. I moved my body in little circles trying to impale myself on his cock, but it kept missing my pussy. So I boldly reached between our bodies to take it in my hand and point its way to my waiting slit. That was another first. I liked the feeling of control it gave me. I rubbed the thick head against my wet opening, coating it thoroughly with my juices before directing it inside. Then, when I felt my pussy lips closing around it, I lowered myself onto him. It slid right in.

From that point on, instinct moved us both. We ground and rolled against each other, each movement rubbing his thick pole against all the sensitive spots inside me. I had a feeling that a dam was about to burst and suddenly found myself drowning in a sea of orgasm that filled my private world. Nothing existed but whirling waves of passion and ecstasy.

When his climax began, I was too preoccupied with my own to even be aware of it. At some point, I know I felt his cock shooting and pulsating inside me, filling me with a torrent of heat that seemed to continue without end. I kept thrusting myself against him, wringing the very last drop from his softening erection, until withered and empty, it slipped from the soft grasp of my pussy's lips.

I don't remember how I got back into my clothes, but somehow I did. Just as I was finishing the last of the buttons, he kissed me lightly on the cheek and said, "Thanks. I'll be sure to ask for you again." He put his robe back on and took some bills out of the pocket. When he handed them to me, I thanked him and thrust them into my purse without stopping to look.

In the elevator on the way down, though, I counted the four fifties. He had given me a two hundred dollar tip. Between that and my share of the three hundred dollar fee, I had enough to buy myself a classy new outfit. Looking at my watch, I saw it was only eight-thirty. I still had half an hour to make it to the shops. I asked the driver to drop me off, and he willingly obliged.

I was wearing my new outfit the next night when Doug got home from work, and he almost didn't notice it. When he finally did, he asked sternly, "Is that a new dress?"

"New for me," I answered. "I got it at a garage sale. Only fifteen dollars."

He smiled with satisfaction. "There's a good girl," he said. "I'm very pleased to see that you're learning how to be creative about money."

"Oh, I'm getting creative, all right," I said. It was hard to keep my face from showing how hard I was laughing at him inside. The whole thing had been a thrill, but I think that putting one over on Doug was the best part of it.

Anyway, that first time was six or seven years ago, and I've been doing it ever since. Not every night, the way Anita does. Not even every week. Only when there's something I especially want.

I like the money, of course, and the things I get to buy with it. I like the vindictive little tremor I get when Doug compliments me on all the good stuff I've been able to get at garage sales. I don't really resent him so much anymore, because I feel like I'm getting even every time I fuck some stranger for money. I don't even mind it when he pokes at me in bed and sticks his cock into me. It's usually over in a few seconds. If it happens to take him longer than that, I amuse myself by thinking about the erotic things I've done with men that he knows nothing about.

But there's more to it than that. I like the feeling I get when somebody hands me money for sucking him off or letting him fuck me. It makes me feel like I'm really worth something. I've become real good at what I do. I like figuring out what it takes to please them, and I like the sounds they make when I get it right. I also like the things most of them do to me. Actually, the only time I ever get off is when I'm doing it for money.

STREETWALK

Walt, thirty-nine, is an architect. His expensively tailored clothing fits him as if it were made right on his body. His dark hair is flecked with silver and looks like it receives daily professional attention, as do his polished nails. Success is written all over him. Even the tall and slender lines of his body suggest the kind of care for which most people have neither the time nor the money. When he talks about his favorite turn-on, however, he exposes another side of himself, a side which the casual observer could not possibly know, a dark side.

Believe it or not, I like to buy it. There's something so sleazy about paying a hooker for sex that the very thought of it gets me hard. It's not the sex, you understand. I can pretty much get that as much as I want, whenever I want it. I've been married twice. In between—I'm in between at the moment—I've had one girlfriend after another. I like women, and they like me. When I'm in a relationship with a woman, it just seems natural for us to have good sex.

But at the beginning of a relationship, even if you both want sex, you have to play the game according to certain fixed rules. First there's dinner, whether you're hungry or not. Then there's the drinking, even if you don't really feel like it. All the time you're wondering, When I take her home will she invite me in? And she's probably wondering the same sort of thing about you.

It's a trial-and-error game. You make a move and watch to see how she's going to respond. Then she makes a move, and you know she's watching your reactions. You're never quite sure where it's going to go. What does she like? What doesn't she like? What will she do? What won't she do? Some people enjoy that courtship dance, but frankly, I don't. For me, it's just a means to an end.

But hookers. Ahh, hookers are something else. With a hooker, there's no uncertainty. You get exactly what you bargain for.

My work takes me out of town a few times a year, usually to faraway cities. I can't tell you how much I look forward to those trips. They ought to be a nuisance because I really can't spare the time away from my work table. Instead, those trips are the highlights of my year. They furnish a spice that changes my whole outlook on life for a while.

If I know I'm going to be in a particular town for three days—which is how long I usually stay—I make plans to pick up a streetwalker on the very last night. That keeps me stimulated the whole time I am there. Every night, after business is finished, I go to the sleaze district, just hanging around and exploring until I feel like part of it.

When I first started traveling, I tried asking hotel concierges where to find what I was looking for. They didn't seem to have any idea. They would make suggestions that usually turned out to be singles bars where the local meat went to look itself over, or they'd give me phone numbers to call.

I think there was a communication problem. I just couldn't make it clear what I really wanted. Don't misunderstand. I tried. It's not that I was embarrassed. With the tips I give those guys, I don't have to be embarrassed about anything. No, it's just that they can't relate to somebody like me looking for the kind of sleaze I am interested in. No matter how bluntly I tried to put it, they just didn't hear what I was asking for.

That didn't stop me, though. I soon became a connoisseur of tenderloins. Put me in any American city and within three hours I'll know what streets the hookers walk at night and where the hotel rooms rent by the half hour. I don't have to tell you how I find places like that. It doesn't matter. If you were interested enough in that part of it, you'd know already. Let's just say I always find them.

I walk slowly along the streets, listening to the sights and looking at the sounds. I soak it up, keeping my eyes and ears open, and in the process, I find things out. You'd be surprised about the variations in hookers' rates from one town to another, for example. By the time my big night comes, I know almost as much about what goes on in the streets as some of the hookers themselves.

They live on those streets. That's where they meet their friends. That's where they find their clients. That's where they negotiate their deals. That's where they eat and breathe.

I love to hear them quoting prices to the johns, especially when they get specific about what they're offering to do. I like hearing their dirty talk. They say things like, "Fifty for a straight fuck; sixty for a blow job; seventy-five for half-and-half." Or, "I don't take it up the ass, but I'll swallow for forty bucks." Or, "Hey, honey, how'dya like to put your dick between my titties."

I get so turned on eavesdropping on that kind of talk that when I get back to my own hotel on the other side of town, I really have to fight the temptation to masturbate for relief. I haven't done that sort of thing since I was a kid. Besides, I prefer to keep my sexual tension building.

The thing I like best about sex with a streetwalker is the idea that it's a completely commercial transaction, like a contract. Before I actually do it, I look at the deal from every possible angle. I decide what kind of girl I want. I may even have a specific one in mind. By then, I've been looking them over for a couple of days.

A lot goes into deciding what I want her to do. I especially like the idea of discussing that with them in the street before doing the deal. I like using street language. "I want a rim job," I'll say. Or, "I want to fuck you doggie-style." Sometimes, I ask a price for something out of the ordinary. Never mind what. It isn't because I really want her to do it; it's just to prolong the bargaining process.

I really love that bargaining process. No matter what I ask for and no matter where I am, it isn't going to cost more than a hundred or so, which doesn't mean a thing to me. But I act like it matters so I can stretch out the negotiation. Usually, by that time, I've gotten a pretty good idea about rates in the neighborhood, so I know how it's going to end up. But getting there is half the fun.

The negotiation is a major part of the turn-on. It's a form of intimate sexual interaction that puts me on the same plane with someone who is about as far away from my world as anyone can possibly get. I make my living—and it's a good one—designing buildings. My work lasts for generations. She makes her living dropping her drawers and spreading her legs. Five seconds of orgasm and whatever she has achieved is gone forever.

The idea that we are absolute strangers talking in the street about the price for a very specific sexual act is so bizarre that it actually becomes part of the whole erotic experience. I mean, think about it. I never spoke to this woman before. I don't even ask her name. If she offers one, it's an obvious fake. The names Easy and Juicy happen to be popular at the moment. But it doesn't matter. It's of no consequence.

The first and only time she and I have any conversation at all, we're talking about doing the most personal and intimate things two people can do. We're discussing the way our bodies are going to meet—the contact our private parts are going to have with each other. We're talking about my penis or her anus or her nipples or my scrotum. And we're connecting the conversation to specific amounts of dollars and cents.

We both know that within five or ten minutes we'll be exposing our sexual parts to each other. I'll be inside her, or she'll have her mouth on me. We both see that in our minds while we stand there on the pavement amidst the garbage cans and traffic.

Most of them—at least the ones I usually pick—are good at negotiating. They have to be specialists at reading human nature. They realize that money isn't really an object with me, but they also understand that for me the negotiation is part of the attraction, part of the sex. They pad their prices enough to make me pay for that particular pleasure, too. Eventually, we reach an agreement and head for one of the revolving-door hotels where somebody knocks on the door if you're not out within thirty minutes.

Now here's something I didn't expect to tell you. As you can see, I'm a meticulous person. Sometimes, I change my shirt three times in the course of a day. I hate anything that isn't absolutely spotless. But when I take a hooker into one of those sleazebag joints, I like it that the sheets weren't changed after the previous customer's visit. If they're stained, so much the better. I even like the musty smell that pervades a room that sunlight never enters because the shades are never opened.

Maybe it's a fetish of some kind. Certainly, my favorite way of doing it follows along with the same theme. I like her to keep her clothes on. Just lift up her skirt or drop her pants around her ankles. I even like it when her underclothing is a little soiled.

I like her to stand up and bend over with her hands on the bed, while I slip in from behind. Sometimes, I keep my pants on the whole time, just opening my fly to get access. I wear a condom, of course, but I really wish I didn't have to. The idea that several men have probably been inside her within the past few hours is also something that turns me on. Usually, the actual contact doesn't last more than a minute or two. Then, as soon as I'm done, I zip up my pants and leave the room without saying good-bye. I never say thanks.

The next day, it's back to real life, which isn't bad at all. I'm seeing two attractive women at the moment, and my life is filled with plenty of passion and intimacy. But with all I've revealed about myself to you, now you know my secret. What really turns me on is paying for swift sleazy sex.

SEE ME

ACCORDING TO THE JUDAIC-CHRISTIAN-ISLAMIC MYTH OF creation, the original human beings lived idyllically in a sublime garden, where everything they needed hung conveniently from trees. Then, one day, they ate the wrong fruit and realized, for the first time, that they were naked. Ashamed, they covered themselves with fig leaves, and that got them expelled from paradise.

Some people say the story is literally true, that the events described in Genesis actually happened. They can even pinpoint the spot where the Garden of Eden was located. Others regard Genesis as a poetic comment on the origin of human consciousness. We won't take a position on that particular controversy. Either way, the tale of the fig leaves proves to be a very accurate characterization of a common human attitude.

In the Arctic, clothes are necessary at all times of the year to keep people from freezing to death. In most other regions, the same is true for certain seasons. During summers in the temperate zones, however, there are plenty of balmy afternoons when clothing is not an aid to survival at all, so we must be donning garments for some other reason.

Even when sleeping, we are likely to wear something to cover our nakedness. Since we usually use blankets for warmth, the pajamas and nightgowns we put on don't really serve any practical purpose. At the beach, swimsuits may actually be a detriment because they slow us down in the water, give sand a place to accumulate, and stay wet long after our bodies have dried. Most of us wear them anyway.

We don't hesitate to televise bloody battles taking place in far corners of the world, displaying human gore and suffering in all its gruesome reality. On the other hand, the flash of a nipple is likely to get a television station's license suspended, particularly if it's shown when children might be watching. Do we really believe that, after exposure to death in all its forms, our offspring will be corrupted or traumatized by seeing the fountain of mammalian life? Or are we unconsciously trying to teach them the same sense of shame we learned from previous generations, even unto the first humans from whom we descend?

Although streaking, flashing, and mooning have all been popular pastimes among twentieth-century youth, upon reaching adulthood, most streakers, flashers, and mooners put aside these childish amusements to adopt society's prevailing attitude. There are a few who visit nudist camps and clothing-optional beaches, but the great majority of American adults regard the naked body as something that should be seen only by a spouse or physician.

Perhaps the fact that almost any exposure is regarded as indecent is the reason why some of the people with whom we spoke said they derived a special kind of excitement from showing their sex organs to others, or even from being watched while having sexual intercourse.

AUDIENCE

Candyce, who is in her early thirties, is a brunette at the moment. She says that her career as a runway model has required her to change her hair's length and color so often that she no longer remembers its original shade. Sometimes, when her dark brown eyes clashed with a garment she was modeling, she even used tinted contacts to change her eye color. She is about 5´10˝ and carries herself with

*an easy grace. Her body, although fashionably slender, is shapely, tending to soft
curves rather than sharp angles.*

I guess I've always been an exhibitionist. I know that's how I got into
modeling at the age of fifteen. Sounds young, but here I am not yet
thirty-five and already over the hill. Designers don't like showing their
lines on old ladies like me. They prefer them young.

Luckily, I was warned about that when I first started, and I was smart
enough to let my father manage my money. He made some good in-
vestments for me, and now I have the capital to start a little business of
my own. I just haven't decided what it's going to be yet. So I'm not worried about money. It's the work I'm going to miss. Modeling is a way
of showing off. I love the chance to dress up and prance for all those
people.

I don't tell this to everyone, but I think what I like best is the frantic
activity in the dressing rooms. Models can't concern themselves with
modesty at a time like that, and it's common for men to walk in and out
of the rooms without anyone giving it a second thought. There are hair-
dressers, makeup artists, designers, assistants, and guys with clipboards
keeping us all on schedule. The myth is that most of them are gay, and
that the straight ones are too interested in business to care about watching us undress. But neither of those stories convinces me.

I've seen them looking at me as I slip out of one outfit and into another, especially when the garments are the clinging kind. Then, of
course, a model can't wear any underwear that might interrupt the flow
of the fabric. So there are times when half the women in the room are
totally nude. That's when the men seem to find the most reasons for
coming in. I don't mind. Actually, I love it.

I've felt that way as long as I can remember, even when I was growing up here in New York City. I had four older brothers. I was the only
girl and a spoiled one at that. My parents were always buying me pretty
new clothes, and I liked watching myself put them on and take them
off. Sometimes, I would deliberately leave my bedroom door open,
hoping that my brothers would see me naked. I'm pretty sure that if

they did, they would have turned away like the gentlemen my parents brought them up to be. But at the time, I would imagine them standing there watching me as I performed before the mirror. So you see, I was an exhibitionist even then.

When I was in junior high school, it seemed natural for me to make up a portfolio and send it to modeling agencies. By the time I was fifteen, I was getting my feet wet in the business. The greatest thrill in the world for me was walking down a runway, turning this way and that, showing myself to a room full of attentive eyes as I demonstrated the swirl of a designer's new skirt.

Just before I turned twenty, my parents retired to south Florida. I was working so steadily in the garment center of New York that I stayed behind and got my own apartment. I missed them and went to visit whenever I could, especially when I was tired or feeling unhappy. They had a lovely house on the beach, and when I needed escape, I went there.

I like the beach, probably for the opportunity it gives me to show off in a dental-floss bikini with a G-string bottom. Naturally, I get new ones every year because I've always got to be in the height of fashion. You can be sure they're always the briefest I can find.

Models aren't supposed to have any tan lines. That justifies my unhooking the top so I can get an even tan on my shoulders and back. If it happens to slip off when I turn over, well, I can't help that.

I met Jesse on the beach. It was about three years ago, just about the time I began to notice that I wasn't getting as many modeling calls as I used to. I was feeling kind of old, and since I didn't have any work lined up for a couple of weeks, I decided to pay my parents a visit. I can always count on them to tell me I look beautiful and to admire my new clothes. Seeing them never fails to pick me up, so I hopped on a jet to Florida.

It was October, and New York was cold, but it was just like summer on the beach near their home. Within a few hours, I was baking away my troubles in the Florida sun. On that particular afternoon, I was busy anointing my breasts with suntan lotion, slipping the oily tips of my fingers into the cups of my bikini bra. It wasn't my fault that my nipples were momentarily exposed in the process.

I could see the men around me stealing glances every time it happened. One of them, a brash young guy with suntanned skin and hair tied back in a ponytail, openly and deliberately looked at me before walking over to where I was seated. He was tall and towered over me for a moment. Sitting down uninvited on my blanket, he smiled and introduced himself. He looked a good ten years younger than I, but his smile was so self-assured that the age difference was easy to forget. "I haven't seen you around here before," he said. "Just moved in?"

When I told him I had come down from New York to visit my parents, he smiled again. "Any boyfriend down here?" he asked.

A little startled by his directness, I said, "Well, no. Not at the moment."

"Great," he said, moving closer and taking my hand. "Come out with me tonight. We'll have some fun."

He wasn't my type at all. Too young, for one thing. Too rough around the edges, for another. But there were two things I liked about him. One was the way he got right to the point, without that beating around the bush that passes for conversation among sophisticated New York yuppies. The other was a little hard for me to comprehend, but it had something to do with the way he had appreciatively looked at my exposed nipples without trying to hide it, while the other men on the beach were shamefacedly sneaking peeks.

So, without really thinking it through, I agreed to meet him on the boardwalk at eight that night. We went to a carnival and really did have fun. The next night we watched some drag races. I wasn't feeling quite so old anymore, and I was flattered that such a young and handsome guy found me attractive, but I knew he was really too young for me.

I had already agreed to go to a movie with him, but I decided that it would be our last date. After the movie, I changed my decision. I think it was *Henry and June,* a film about two controversial writers whose work is supposed to be shockingly erotic. To be perfectly frank with you, I haven't read them, but the movie certainly had some erotic scenes in it.

During one of them, Jesse put his arm around my shoulders and began kissing my neck. I guessed the sex on screen was getting to him. I knew it was getting to me. I hadn't made out in a movie theater since I was a teenager, but it seemed perfectly natural for me to respond when he pressed his lips to mine. As his tongue darted in and out of my mouth, I felt his hand slipping under my skirt.

His fingertips stroked lightly at the insides of my thighs, moving higher as our kiss intensified. I felt myself getting damp between the legs as his hand brushed confidently across the crotch of my panties. My desire mounted while his fingers explored. Involuntary movements of my hips propelled me forward, against his hand. I was vaguely aware of the people sitting all around us, but that only heightened my excitement.

The tip of one finger found its way inside my panties to sample the moisture of my sex, while his other hand began petting and fondling my breasts through the light blouse I had on. I wasn't wearing a bra, and I could feel my nipples stiffening as he rolled each of them slowly. Then, while our lips were still locked in a passionate kiss, he unbuttoned the front of my blouse. It happened so fast that I didn't even know it until the material fell back, exposing my breasts.

He kissed each of them, trailing the tip of his tongue over my nipples. Something similar was happening on the screen, and I watched it for a moment while Jesse's lips made me tingle. I knew that some of the people around us were looking at us instead of the movie. This wasn't like getting undressed in the changing room while men walked in and out. At least that had an air of legitimacy. Here I was sitting in a public place allowing strangers not only to see my naked breasts, but to see Jesse freely handling and licking them. What a wonderful forbidden thrill!

Closing my eyes tightly, I imagined the people staring at me and becoming sexually aroused by my passions. I realized that being the center of their attention was even more exciting to me than the things Jesse was doing. As he sucked on one erect nipple, I moaned. I'm not sure whether it was a sincere expression of my feelings, or an unconscious way of attracting an even bigger audience.

Even though my eyes were closed, I could tell from the music that the movie was drawing to an end. The theater lights would come on any minute. I began to panic, because being on display was turning me on so much that I was afraid I wouldn't be able to stop. Jesse saved me. As the final credits rolled across the screen, he slowly, almost mockingly, rebuttoned my blouse and smoothed my skirt. He seemed to be taking as much pleasure in covering me as he had in exposing me.

When we left the theater, we were both so aroused that we pulled into a quiet parking lot and made love in the back seat of Jesse's car. I grew up in New York City, and that's not really a New York thing. It was something I had never done before. I liked it, but although Jesse's thrusting was deep and satisfying, we weren't able to recapture the intensity we had both felt in the movie theater.

That night, I think I realized for the first time just how much of an exhibitionist I am. I suspect that Jesse understood it all along. Anyway, I thought about him all that night and about the thrill he had given me in the movie theater. I found myself looking forward to seeing him again. It was exciting to be with him because he was an exhibitionist, too. It might have been the only thing we had in common, but to be perfectly frank with you, it was enough to keep me interested in him for quite a while.

The next night we were going out dancing. On the way, Jesse told me he had to make a little detour. He said his friend Andy, whom I had met on the beach a few days earlier, was out of town for a while. Jesse had promised to go over and water the plants.

When we got to Andy's house, I was surprised at how nicely it was decorated, especially for a bachelor. The living room furniture was tasteful and expensive, and the thick white carpet was so luxurious that I slipped out of my shoes as soon as we entered. I asked Jesse if he'd like help in his watering tasks, but without a word, he took me in his arms and kissed me long and hard.

He was very good at it, and I became lost in swirling emotions as his hands possessed my body. Slowly, we sank to the floor without interrupting the kiss or breaking the embrace. Expertly, Jesse managed to undress me. Before I knew it, we were both completely nude, our hungry bodies pressed together on the carpet.

His hands were all over me, gently squeezing my breasts and softly stroking my bare belly and buttocks. I reached for him and held his penis in my hand for the first time. I was surprised at how thick and rigid it felt.

He teased me with his fingertips, running them gently through my pubic hair and dipping them lightly into my vagina for a moment, before moving on to stroke other, less sensitive, parts of my body. Then, back again to my labia, pinching gently and suddenly flitting away, like a will-o'-the-wisp. I tried to press his hand against me, to let him know how much I wanted his fingers inside me, but he remained in control.

Involuntarily, my bare legs began spreading wider and wider, silently inviting him to invade me. He continued teasing me by lightly touching my wetness, carrying some of it to my nipples and rubbing them in a circular motion. I begged him with my moans, drawing my knees back to open myself to him even more. When he began brushing the skin of my thighs with his lips, I sighed in hungry pleasure. He moved higher, nuzzling my vulva, tasting my juices with the very tip of his tongue, and kissing my parted labia.

I moaned and squeezed my eyes tightly shut with passion. He lapped at my sex, bathing my sexual parts with the soft touch of his tongue. His throaty, guttural moans blended with mine to fill the air with erotic harmony. When he started sucking on my clitoris, pangs of erotic desire lifted me even higher. I wanted to see what he was doing, to watch his tongue on my slit, to see his face as he made oral love to me, so I opened my eyes just a little, peeking out from between slightly parted lids.

There was Andy, sitting on the sofa and staring intently at us. I shut my eyes again, thinking that maybe it was just my imagination providing an audience to increase my pleasure. Slowly, I opened them, wide this time, so I would know for sure. Yes. He was there. He was not a figment of my imagination. Here I was spread out on his living room floor while his friend lapped at my sex. I was totally nude and totally vulnerable.

It was wrong for a thousand reasons. But instead of feeling uneasy, as I should have, I became even more excited. He was an audience, watching me doing the most personal and intimate things anyone can possibly do, and that turned me on.

I felt I was performing for him. My sex was completely open to his gaze. His eyes were fixed on my vulva, watching Jesse's tongue dart in and out of me, seeing my tissues redden. My juices flowed as I observed him observing me. His eyes didn't meet mine, but I kept looking at him and getting hotter. I didn't know what to do. For a fleeting moment, I thought of closing my eyes again and pretending not to know he was there, but I couldn't bring myself to look away. I saw that I was turning him on, and that was turning me on. I struggled to fight back the climax that was building in my loins.

Andy was leaning back on the couch, intent on the sight of what Jesse was doing to my naked body. The front of Andy's pants bulged, and I noticed his hand straying unconsciously to his groin. His face wore a hypnotized look. I was positively thrilled that the sight of my body could have such a stimulating effect on him. It was like the thrill I got in the movie theater, only ten times better.

Andy's fingers fumbled with the zipper of his pants and extracted his fully erect penis. Still staring at my sex, he began stroking his own, making it turn a shiny purple color. I stared at the huge organ. "Oooh," I groaned, wanting to be sure that he knew that I knew he was there.

At the sound, he glanced toward my face and our eyes locked. Deliberately, I looked at his penis, wanting to give him the same thrill his attention was giving me. Jesse's tongue was still lapping at my clitoris. I couldn't tell whether he knew of Andy's presence, but that didn't matter. All I cared about were the indescribable sensations flashing through my body.

I knew I wouldn't be able to hold back the climax anymore. I wanted

Andy to see me come. I let him hear my rhythmic groans, watching as his hand flew even faster up and down the length of his penis. I rocked my hips, thrusting my wet vulva hard against Jesse's hungry mouth and using my body language to let him and Andy know that I was about to go off.

Then, uttering a loud animal groan, I began to orgasm. I glanced into Andy's eyes to be sure they were on me. Then I looked at his penis in time to see it erupt, knowing that his fountain of hot liquid had been inspired by me. I almost screamed as I reached the peak of the most powerful climax I had ever experienced.

As I slid down from the summit, I felt Jesse mount me and slide his erection into my receptive vulva. I closed my eyes and focused on his thrusts, knowing that Andy was still on the couch, watching us as his own orgasm wound down. Jesse's penis grew thicker inside me, preparing to spurt. I remember wishing Andy could see what I was feeling inside.

Jesse and I lay in each other's arms for a few silent minutes. Then, just as Jesse rolled over onto the floor beside me, his friend rose from his seat. "Oops, I guess I got home too soon," he said. He left the house without another word.

Jesse and I dressed quickly and left, too. We understood each other completely. I realized Jesse must have known that Andy was not out of town. He must have prearranged the whole thing with his friend, thinking he would have to trick me into performing with him for a live audience. But there was no more need for subtlety. There was no denying that putting on the show for Andy had turned me on.

After that, Jesse arranged other audiences for our lovemaking. One night, we hot-tubbed with two gay women who were friends of his. They seemed to get a real thrill out of watching Jesse and me have uninhibited sex in the heated water. Another night, we went on a double date with Jesse's roommate and the roommate's girlfriend. We ended up back at their apartment, each couple watching the other get it on.

I went back to New York a few weeks later. After that, Jesse and I got together whenever I was in Florida visiting my parents. Eventually, though, we fell out of touch. I haven't seen or heard from him in quite a while.

I'm dating someone in New York, now, and we've a commitment to each other. To be perfectly frank with you, our sex life is pretty conventional, and I find it unsatisfying. I nurse the hope that some day I'll be able to let him know about my secret streak of exhibitionism. Maybe I'll even be able to get him interested in the kind of sex that turns me on the most.

Every now and then, when I think of the exceptionally erotic adventures that I had with Jesse, I wish I hadn't lost touch with him. I have to admit that even after all this time, whenever I go to visit my parents, I find myself looking for him on the beach and remembering the thrill of being watched while he made love to me. I wonder if I'll ever experience anything that exciting again.

REFLECTIONS

Russell, forty-six, is well tanned from time spent outdoors staring into tide pools or hanging over the rails of a boat. He is of average height and of medium build. His snowy hair is moderately long and combines with a serious expression to give him a quiet look of dignity. He stops frequently to clean his gold-rimmed glasses, using them as a prop in conversation. Sometimes, his words sound like part of a lecture. Russell teaches oceanography to graduate students.

There are lots of resources in that big old puddle, so there's money to be made in oceanography, but not by teaching it. Teaching brings a different kind of satisfaction. There's a special kind of excitement I feel when I stand up in front of the room with fifteen or twenty pairs of eyes glued to my every move. It's almost sexual. I'm an exhibitionist. There's no doubt about that.

Exhibiting myself is the greatest turn-on of all. Unfortunately, my wife doesn't really understand this. Our sex is good, but what turns me on doesn't necessarily turn her on. When I get undressed, I'd really like her to look at me, but she hardly pays attention. I'd like to have her watch me masturbate, but she just laughs at that suggestion, so I don't push it any further.

Since my wife won't cooperate, I'm always looking to find other outlets for my exhibitionism. Recently, I've been displaying myself to the woman who moved into the house next door. I met her once, but I don't really know her. All I know is she's a rather young and attractive single parent. I'm not even sure of her name.

One morning, when I had just stepped out of the shower, I discovered that she was watching me. A mirror phenomenon brought her gaze to my attention. I was standing naked in front of the bathroom mirror when I noticed that it reflected the bedroom mirror through the open door. The doubly reflected image showed me the window of the neighbor's house.

Her blinds were closed, but I could clearly see a face peering out between two slats that were being held open. It was my neighbor, observing me by way of the double reflection and apparently unaware that I could see her as clearly as she could see me. I stood, dripping wet, and watched her in my bathroom mirror.

I assumed that she just had been looking out the window and caught me in the nude. I took advantage of the situation by stalling. Instead of wrapping myself in a towel to dry off as I ordinarily would, I stayed wet and naked while I combed my hair and brushed my teeth. When I was ready to get dressed, I saw that she was still watching.

I thought about the experience as I drove to the university that day, hoping she had enjoyed watching me as much as I enjoyed showing off. I wondered whether her voyeurism was the result of a happy coincidence or whether she had watched me before. A mild form of sexual stimulation stayed with me for the rest of the day. When I went to sleep that night, I found myself looking forward to my shower of the morrow.

The following morning, I woke up with a feeling of sexual anticipation that stayed with me during my shower. I felt like hurrying through it to see whether she would be there, but I am a man of regular habits and stayed under the hot spray for my full seven minutes.

When I got out, I stood naked before the bathroom mirror again, trying to appear casual as I positioned myself in a way that would allow me to catch the double reflection. I was partially erect already, but when I saw her face peering at me from between the blinds, I came to full rigidity. I hoped she had a good view.

I realized then that she had figured out my routine and was familiar with my schedule. I wondered how long she had been watching me. How many times had she seen me before? The idea bothered me. Not because I resented her spying, but because if I had been aware of it sooner, I could have been enjoying it every morning and experiencing the intense turn-on it gave me.

That time I showed her more than I had the day before. I made sure to bend over several times to retrieve imaginary items from the cabinet beneath the sink, giving her a full moon whenever possible. I fiddled around for a while with a bottle of cologne. I held my genitals up with one hand as I sprinkled talcum over myself, something I don't usually do. I didn't tear myself away until I started to fear that I was being obvious. If she knew that I knew, she might not watch me anymore.

That night, I kept grabbing my wife's bottom and insisting we go to bed early. We made love twice, and I think I would have been ready for another, if she hadn't made some crack about my being unusually aroused. I was afraid if I showed too much excitement, she would be able to figure out my little secret.

The next morning it took all my willpower to stay in the shower for the usual time. When I got out, I knew, without bothering to check the mirror, that my young neighbor was at her observation post. I toweled myself quickly and then pranced around the room in all my erect glory. I was so excited that it hurt. Without thinking about it, I stroked my erection in sympathy with its discomfort. Then I realized that she must be seeing that, too, and that made me ache all the more.

I started going through the motions of masturbation, rubbing myself up and down rhythmically with one hand and cupping my scrotum with the other. I kept my eye on the mirror the whole time, watching myself and watching her watch me. I thought I was only doing it for her to see, but I soon felt a climax coming on.

I was going to let my neighbor see my orgasm, but I found myself craving my wife's body again, so I ran straight to the bed and mounted her without ceremony. She was still half-asleep, but she smiled delightedly and hummed her approval as I entered her. It was swift, but wonderful. I couldn't remember being that stimulated in a long time. When I returned to the bathroom to clean myself up before getting dressed, I noticed that my neighbor was gone.

Since then, morning exhibitions for my surreptitious observer have become part of my daily routine. I think it's taken about ten years off my age. My wife can't get over my newfound sexual energy. I wish I could tell her where it's coming from, but I know she wouldn't approve, and I wouldn't want to have to give it up. As long as it isn't hurting anyone, why shouldn't I enjoy this wonderful, wonderful turn-on?

RESEARCH

Millie, thirty-nine, is a lab technician. She stands about 5´3´´, with a medium frame and dark eyes to match her curly brown hair. Her husband, Jeff, is an electrician. We met Millie and Jeff when they agreed to participate in research we are doing for an upcoming book. Several weeks later, Millie called to thank us for the greatest turn-on she had ever experienced. We asked her to describe it. She stammered for a moment and said she wasn't sure she could talk to us about it. Then she said, "I know what I'll do. I'll talk as if it weren't really you in that room with us, but some other researchers."

It all began when Jeff came home with a newspaper and showed me an ad he had seen in the personals column. The people who ran the ad said they were authors of books on sexuality. They were gathering material and looking for couples who would be willing to permit observation of their sexual activities.

We laughed at the idea of people having sex while being watched by researchers with clipboards and white coats. How ridiculous! But we didn't laugh long, because Jeff started getting frisky, and the next thing I knew, we were having a quickie right there on the kitchen floor.

For the next couple of days, Jeff brought up the subject regularly. He had kept the newspaper and would take it out, point to the ad, and begin imagining what a research session would be like. It was kind of fun to fantasize about doing it, and we seemed to be having more and more sex as a result. Both of us must have been stimulated by the idea because every time we started talking about it, we wound up in the sack.

One evening, in the middle of the conversation, Jeff picked up the newspaper and reached for the phone. Playfully, he said, "I'm going to call them."

At first, I thought he was kidding, but then he actually started to dial. I figured he was expecting me to stop him, and I decided I wasn't going to give him that satisfaction. I guess I wanted to see how far he would go before hanging up.

When he spoke into the phone, saying, "I'm calling about the ad," I thought he was putting me on. I didn't realize he was serious until I saw how nervous he seemed to be. "Yes," he continued. "The ad about sex research." He was silent for a while, nodding his head as the person at the other end gave some sort of explanation. There was an intent look on his face when he said, "OK. I'll have to talk to my wife and get back to you."

When he hung up the phone, he said, "Well, they sound legitimate to me." I couldn't believe my ears.

He told me that the people who ran the ad were a husband-and-wife research team. They had written several books about sex and were planning a new one, in which they would describe the sexual behavior of real live people, based completely on observations that they themselves had made.

They promised that the entire process would be professional and that identities of participants would be kept in strictest confidence. They lived in the same city as we and had suggested that we meet them some place for a drink or a cup of coffee. That way, we could decide whether we felt comfortable enough to go any further.

When Jeff began telling me all that, I started to giggle, but I soon realized that he was dead serious. "Wait a minute," I said. "You don't really think I'd be willing to let two absolute strangers watch us get undressed and make love, do you? No way. That's a very private thing."

"Well, this wouldn't exactly be public," he answered. "There are only two of them. It's like scientific research." Then in a quieter voice, he added, "Besides, I think it could be very exciting. It's something we've never done before, and I'm sure we'd never do it again. I think it would be a real turn-on for me, for both of us, if we don't allow our inhibitions to get in the way."

"No," I said. "This is too weird. Talking about it is one thing, but doing it is another."

Jeff persisted. "There can't be any harm in getting acquainted with them," he insisted. "We can always say no."

I had to admit he had a point. Eventually, I agreed to meet them for coffee. I had three reasons. Mainly, I wanted to please Jeff. Our sex life was good, but after twelve years of marriage, it occurred to me that maybe he was feeling a need for something different, and I didn't want him to go looking for it on the outside. Also, as a lab tech, I was able to tell myself that we might actually be making some kind of contribution to scientific understanding. I remembered reading that Masters and Johnson had watched people having sex before they wrote their book on the subject. Finally, I must admit, I also thought it might be a turn-on.

When we went to a cafe to meet with the researchers—let's call them John and Mary—I felt a little more comfortable about things. For one thing, they were middle-aged. And they were polite without being syrupy. I didn't feel the least bit threatened by them. They were warm and friendly, and even though they spoke quite professionally and seriously about the research they were doing, they weren't stuffy or overly technical about it, either. They even made us feel that the project would be fun.

The fact that they were a married couple themselves made it easier also. They understood how nervous we felt and suggested that, with the kids away at camp, we would probably be most comfortable in our own surroundings. If I was going to try to please Jeff by doing something like this, I didn't think I could pick a better couple to do it with.

We left, telling them that we'd think it over and call them if we decided to go through with it. By the time we got home, I had already made up my mind. We were going to do it. We phoned immediately to say we were willing and invited them to come and observe us the following night.

I'll never forget the way I felt the next day at work. I could not keep my mind on my job no matter how hard I tried. I kept thinking about what would be going on later that night and wondering if I would really go through with what I had committed myself to do. I had to leave work early, just to keep from having an accident in the lab.

I started getting ready as soon as I got into the house. I felt really strange as I showered, realizing that within a couple of hours two strangers would be looking at my naked body. I think I took extra care to scrub myself for that reason. While dressing, I found myself attempting to select my prettiest and sexiest underwear. There was no doubt about it, I was fascinated by our participation in the research. I'll confess that, even though I worked in the world of science and was about to be a research subject, my thoughts were not entirely scientific.

Jeff got home just as I was slipping into a pair of lacy black panties. He leered at me and winked, saying, "Oh, yes, they're going to like you in those." By that time, I was actually trembling so much that I had to ask him to snap the matching bra.

Jeff got ready more quickly than I. We sat on the couch in the living room, waiting for the researchers and trying to control our emotions. I could tell by the way Jeff kept licking his lips and stammering that he was as nervous as I. We made idle conversation that somehow never included mention of what we were about to do.

When the doorbell rang, I felt a moment of panic, but it was too late to back out. I opened the door, and John and Mary came in smiling, greeting us warmly. Their presence calmed me a little. Somehow, reality is always a little less terrifying than the anticipation of it.

I felt that I had to play hostess and so I asked if they'd like a glass of wine. I think maybe I needed it to steady myself, anyway. The four of us sat and chatted about the weather or something while we sipped. I could not imagine how we were ever going to move from this superficial socializing to the real business of the evening, but they seemed to be old hands at it.

"I'm sure you're nervous," Mary said. "But, look, the idea is for you to act as natural as possible, as if we weren't here. Just proceed the way you would if you were home by yourselves and making love the way you usually do. Would that be here? Or in the bedroom?"

My throat was too dry to form words, but Jeff answered. "Well, we do it in here sometimes," he said, "but usually we go into the bedroom."

Gracefully, Mary stood. "Well, OK, then," she said. "Which way to your bedroom?"

"Why don't you grab one of those dining room chairs," Jeff said to John, "and I'll take one for your wife." The men carried the chairs into the bedroom while Mary and I followed.

"Maybe this would be easier," Jeff said, "if we just got right to it. I'm going to take off my clothes." With that, he pulled his shirt over his head and began unbuckling his belt. I looked at him, understanding that in a moment he would be undressed and then all eyes in the room would be on me. Instinctively, I undressed as quickly as I could.

As I unzipped and removed my dress, I looked at the floor, too embarrassed to make eye contact with the strangers, so I'm not sure whether anybody was watching me at all. With shaking fingers, I unsnapped my bra and wriggled out of it, realizing as I did so that my breasts were fully exposed to these people whom I had met only once before and then only for a few minutes. I could feel my face reddening, but there was no turning back. Still looking down, I unceremoniously stripped off the panties I had so carefully selected just a little earlier.

Now, completely nude, I looked toward Jeff for the first time. He was lying naked on the bed, waiting for me. His penis was fully erect. I don't remember ever seeing it get so hard so quickly. In spite of my embarrassment, I felt my nipples hardening and my vulva becoming moist. I'm not sure whether his excitement was contagious or whether the presence of the two strangers had already inflamed me.

Careful not to look at them, I moved toward the bed. Jeff stared at me, as though he, too, were trying to forget about the presence of the two researchers. He reached for my hand and guided it to his erection. As my fingers closed around its length, I eased myself onto the bed beside him.

I stroked him up and down a few times, feeling awkward and incompetent. I just didn't know what to do next. Then Jeff put his arms around me and pulled me to him, crushing his lips to mine in the most passionate kiss I can ever remember. I closed my eyes tight, losing myself in my husband's embrace, all the time exquisitely aware that everything we did was being watched.

I pressed my entire naked body against my husband's, feeling his erection urgently pressing against my belly. His nipples were as hard as mine and were drilling into the softness of my swelling bosom. I started to wrap my legs around him, but stopped suddenly, realizing that in doing so I was spreading my thighs and presenting the observers with an unobstructed view of my open vagina.

Although my first impulse was to snap my legs together, I didn't. Rather than embarrassment, I was feeling mounting excitement. When I did open my legs, it was deliberate. I imagined the sight I was giving these two perfect strangers. I felt less inhibited and somewhat proud of flaunting my nudity. My husband had always praised the look of my rosy pink nipples, and with his complete permission, I was displaying them to others. Jeff also loves my thick and curling patch of pubic hair, and I wanted to show that to them, too.

I rolled onto my back beside Jeff, and as if he read my mind, Jeff rolled onto his back, too. He reached for the wetness between my legs, moving my thighs further apart with his hand. As I clutched at his long and swollen penis, I kept my eyes tightly shut. When his finger began spreading my labia, I slowly stroked him up and down.

Our hips undulated simultaneously, imitating the movements of intercourse while we lovingly stroked each other's genitals. I felt myself becoming wetter and wetter and heard Jeff groaning with excitement.

The strangers in the room were improving our sex experience and increasing the intensity of our passion, to my surprise.

I wanted them to watch me do everything with Jeff. I wanted to impress them. Maybe I even wanted to turn them on. Grabbing Jeff's penis, I pulled him on top of me. I spread my legs wide and directed his erection to the opening of my sex. I could feel the tip penetrating me and found myself hoping that our visitors had a good clear view so they could see his entry. My vagina got wetter and wetter as he slowly delved deeper and deeper.

I couldn't wait any longer to be filled with the mass of his penis. I flung my hips up at him, jamming my pubic mound against his and forcing him to plunge all the way inside. I issued moans and groans of passion, knowing that every sound could be heard by the two strangers. A sexual fever burned in my chest, leaving me panting with burgeoning desire. My mind filled with perversely erotic ideas.

Directing our movements with the subtle pressure of his legs and arms, Jeff rolled us over so that I was riding him. I lifted myself slowly, aware that the researchers were in a perfect position to see him sliding in and out of me. I found myself performing for them, raising my hips high in the air to give them an even better view.

I remembered a position we used when we were younger and wanted to try it again. Without letting Jeff slide out of me, I squatted over him, the soles of my feet pressing into the mattress as I bobbed up and down on his stiffness. I felt full of boundless energy and the most intense excitement I can ever remember. I knew that they could see the muscles of my buttocks contracting and relaxing as I raised and lowered myself onto him. I perched on the edge of orgasm, but knew that I would not tumble until I willed it.

Slowly, I rotated on Jeff's erection until, still squatting over him, I turned to face John and Mary. Deliberately, I opened my eyes. The observers were seated in the chairs directly in front of me, both of them staring intently at our display. They had a complete view of the front of my naked body and of my open vagina with my husband's penis penetrating it. Neither moved or spoke, but I could see that they were both affected by our performance. That turned me on even more.

I lowered myself into a sitting position and then fell forward. Now I was on my hands and knees between Jeff's legs. His penis was still inside me, and I was still facing the researchers. If Jeff lifted his head slightly and opened his eyes, he would be able to watch my vulva engulfing his erection. And I could watch John and Mary watching us. I humped forward and back, forcing Jeff's penis deep into me and then sliding it almost all the way out. He lay still, giving me complete control of our movements.

I rocked forward, allowing his penis to slip out of me. He groaned audibly, but I raised my backside into the air, posing for him in the doggie position, inviting him to enter me from behind. I knew that he too would be looking at John and Mary as he knelt behind me and aimed his erection at my dripping opening. When he found it, he drove forward in one quick plunge, penetrating me to the utmost and bringing a gasp of passionate pleasure from my lips.

I felt bolder now and actually smiled at John and Mary while Jeff drove in and out. His labored breathing thundered through the room. I added my moans to the sound. I could tell that Jeff was at his height of passion. Our sex had never been this hot or heavy before. I knew that he was going to have a climax, and I wanted to have mine at the same time. The idea of having them watch us simultaneously orgasm was tremendously arousing.

I didn't want it to end, though, until they had seen us having oral sex. I wanted them to watch us doing sixty-nine. I wanted their eyes on Jeff's penis as it slid into my hungry mouth and on my vulva as his tongue explored it.

I pulled away from Jeff and used my hands to position him on his back, with his head toward the observers. I knelt beside his hip and leaned over, running the tip of my tongue over the tip of his penis. As I tasted my own juices on him, I found myself concentrating on the sight I was presenting. Slowly, I engulfed his glans in my mouth, exaggerating the movements of my tongue as I ran it over the swollen organ.

Letting him slip from between my lips, I turned and straddled his head, waving my crotch directly over his face and breathing my hot breath on his quivering penis. I knew that I was giving the two researchers the same view of my vulva that I was giving Jeff. Slowly, I lowered my wet opening until I could feel his lips touching the sensitive membranes. At the same time, I sucked him into my mouth.

Involuntarily, my eyes closed in bliss as we shared the excitement of mutual oral stimulation. I felt my fluids flowing into my husband's sucking mouth, and I felt his manhood pulsating in mine. We licked and lapped at each other for what seemed like forever, both of us aware of our silent observers.

It had been a long time since we were able to do so many different things without giving in to orgasmic release, but it couldn't go on much longer. Finally, when I thought neither of us would be able to stand another moment of the wonderful fascinating torture, I pulled away and turned around, mounting my husband and letting his erection find its way into me once again. I lowered myself onto him, just as his penis started the jerky throbbing that signaled the beginning of his orgasm. When I felt the first jet of hot semen pumping into me, my climax began. We moaned and we groaned and we sang and we roared, both knowing that there was an audience for our music, and both raised to incredible heights by that knowledge.

The orgasm seemed to go on forever. When it finally ended, we were both too spent to move or even to speak. At last, I opened my eyes to see John and Mary rising from their chairs. "Thanks," Mary said. "That was wonderful. Why don't you just relax. We'll find our way out."

Jeff and I lay in each other's arms, listening to the sounds the observers made as they left our home. When they were gone, Jeff kissed me passionately on the lips. Incredibly, I felt myself becoming aroused again. Jeff, too. Before I knew it, he had rolled on top of me and was thrusting his hard penis into me once more. We pumped against each other in a staccato rhythm that ended in another orgasm within seconds.

When it was over, we lay side by side, whispering to each other as we relived the erotic adventure. It wasn't long before we made love again, and again. In fact, we had more sex that night than in any other night either of us could remember.

There was something incredibly exciting about making love in the presence of others. It's an opportunity that doesn't come along every day, and I don't imagine we'll ever get to do it again. But it was such a turn-on that Jeff and I talk about it often, especially when the kids are away and we're preparing ourselves for a night of sexual bliss.

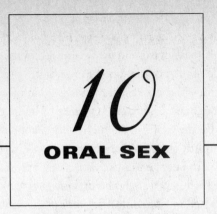

10
ORAL SEX

PHILOSOPHERS HAVE ALWAYS BEEN INTERESTED IN WHY people behave the way they do. Psychology, the formal study of human behavior, did not achieve recognition as a science until the late nineteenth century, however. Since then, a series of psychologists and psychiatrists, beginning with Sigmund Freud, have been propounding theories of personality development. Freud recognized four stages—oral, anal, phallic, and genital—in which conflicts were likely to shape the personality forever.

Many subsequent writers have disagreed with all or part of the Freudian theory. One of these, F. S. Perls, suggested that most major personality development results from attitudes regarding use of the mouth. Perls argued that since life depends on nourishment, and nourishment depends on how we use our lips, teeth, and tongues, early conflicts between our oral desires and the demands of our environment shape the bulk of our subsequent development.

Perhaps Perls's theory explains why so many of our informants reported being particularly turned on by oral sex. In the nineteen forties, the research of Alfred Kinsey and his team established that a great percentage of people in our society have practiced oral sex at some time, and that many practice it on a regular basis. Subsequent research suggests that Kinsey's statistics may have been rather low.

Since we aren't sociologists and made no attempt to gather data from a random sample of the population, we are not in a position to quibble with the projections of those researchers who think they have. Our information is anecdotal rather than statistical. Almost everyone we interviewed found some erotic excitement in oral contact.

Because the mouth plays such an important role in our survival, it is richly endowed with nerve endings that make it extremely receptive to sensation. Since kissing is usually the first intimate contact two people have with each other, most people discover oral sensuality early in their sexual experimentation. Some take it far beyond the mouth-to-mouth kiss.

In this chapter we include the stories of three people who say that oral-genital contact is their greatest turn on. These stories are only a few of the many we received—enough to fill a separate book. We chose them because of their diversity. Murray likes to have oral sex performed on him, while Manny feels that his ability to perform it on a woman is what gives him value as a man. Lonnie enjoys receiving cunnilingus so much that she finds herself thinking about it while engaging in genital intercourse.

MYSTERY LADY

Murray says he has been divorced three times and is working on his seventh serious girlfriend. He carries his sixty years with pride, explaining that he exercises an hour and a half a day to stay fit and preserve his youth. He says that he doesn't put smoke in his lungs or alcohol in his liver and is careful about what he puts in his stomach. Then, with the trace of a smile, he adds that he must be doing something right because he never has a problem finding women.

All the women in my life have been good-looking, and they were all good sex partners. Sex is very important to me. I like everything, but since you asked, oral sex is what turns me on the most. Maybe that's because my first real sex experience was a blow job. It was so unbelievably good that I still think about it, even after forty years.

I was almost nineteen. I know, by today's standards, that was pretty late in life to lose my virginity, but things were different then. Yeah, I petted with girls at parties and necked in the back seat of my car like most of the kids I went to high school with, but that was as far as it went. Lots of my friends talked about getting laid as if they were doing it all the time. I suppose I believed them back then, but as I reflect on it now, I realize that most of their boasting was bullshit.

Anyway, I had been out of high school for a little more than a year. I knew a few girls and went out on a few dates, but I had no sex life at all, unless you count jerking off now and then. I had enlisted in the army and was working in a grocery store while waiting for induction.

One day I was delivering a grocery order to a house that seemed a little familiar. As I pulled the station wagon to the curb, I tried to remember why I recognized it. Then, while I was carrying the groceries up the walk, I recalled that the house had been a legend when I was in high school. The guys all said that the woman who lived there was a sex fiend, that she'd blow anybody who came to her door. They used to say she'd suck off the postman if he brought her a special delivery letter.

None of us really believed it because we couldn't imagine that any woman could be like that, but it was such an exciting idea that we all pretended to believe it. Some of the fellows thought they might have seen her, but nobody was sure. We'd talk about the mystery lady for hours, each of us imagining himself to be the lucky beneficiary of her amazing perversion.

All of this flashed through my head as I approached the front door of the house. At that stage in my life, it didn't take much to turn me on, and the memories of that old rumor were having an effect on me. The grocery bags I carried made me helpless. By the time I rang the doorbell, I had the beginning of a hard-on. When she opened the door, I had to shift the position of my legs to conceal it.

The sight of her made total concealment impossible, though. She was about twice my age, but—even by my immature standards—she was a knockout. She had a head of thick red hair that looked like it wanted to be grabbed with both hands. Her cheekbones were high, giving her face a passionate look. The bright red of her lipstick made her mouth scrumptiously sensual.

I'll never forget her tits! She was wearing a burgundy robe that reached almost to the floor. To my amazement, it was completely open in front, and her big round boobs were in full view. I couldn't take my eyes off them, or off her big red nipples. I was vaguely aware that her muff was showing, too, but I hadn't yet looked directly at it.

When I realized that I was staring, I flushed with embarrassment. My dick was so hard that there was nothing I could do to hide it. All I could think was that I had to get rid of those grocery bags and get the hell out of there in a hurry. I started to stammer something unintelligible, when she reached out and placed her hand on the front of my pants, where my hard-on was sticking way out. My face caught fire.

"Why don't you come in," she said, in a voice that was sexier than I ever could have imagined. "I'll take care of that for you." She gave it a little squeeze.

I was too overwhelmed to process her words. Numbly, I stepped in as she pulled the front door shut. She pointed to a small table in the entry hall, and I obediently put the packages down on it without really understanding what was going on. Grabbing me by the front of my pants again, she walked backwards, pulling me after her into the living room.

She sat on a couch, parting her knees until I could see the red gash of her pussy. Before I even realized it, she unbuckled my belt. My pants had a button fly, but she opened all the buttons at once by pulling the two flaps apart with a swift movement of her hands. Inserting her thumbs inside the waistbands, she pulled my pants and my briefs down at the same time, until they bound my ankles together.

My cock was standing straight out in front of me, trembling as if in disbelief. This couldn't really be happening. It was impossible. It had to be a dream. I watched in a trance as she cradled my strong young pecker in her hands. She drew me to her, bringing the tip of my cock closer to her face. She stared, glassy-eyed, as though mine was the first cock she had ever seen.

I looked down at her, but she never looked up at me. My dick was all she cared about. As far as she knew, it was the only thing that existed. She looked at it in awe, the way a savage would look at a carved wooden idol. There was a connection between her and the penis that only she could possibly understand. She probably didn't understand it, either.

She opened her mouth wide and breathed a blast of hot air over the swollen bulb. Then she puckered up her lips and placed a hot wet kiss right on the tip. The sight of that bright ring of lipstick on the end of my cock turned me on even more, if that was possible.

Her gestures were dramatic and exciting, but that wasn't why she did them. She might have known that I was watching, but it didn't matter to her. In her mind, my only excuse for living was to bring that dick to her door.

She began taking it slowly, almost reverently, into her mouth. A placid look of bliss came over her face as my cock worked its way past her pomegranate red lips. She gurgled slightly as she swallowed its length. The vibrations in her throat stimulated me, making my trigger throb and jump in her mouth. Her tongue swept the underside, her palate caressed the head. All the while, her hands added to the sensation by stroking my balls or circling my prick at its base.

I felt myself bump against the opening to her throat, but she kept taking me deeper. There was a moment of resistance, and then I seemed to enter another universe. Her larynx opened to receive me and closed around the end of my cock to squeeze it tight. She took me deep into her throat. I heard her hot breath hiss through her nostrils and felt it blasting over me as her head bobbed up and down.

Her eyes closed as she descended into a world all her own, a place unknown to me or anyone else. Her mouth and throat produced rhythmic rings of pressure that rippled up and down the length of my cock. Each time her head drew back, I could see thick veins pulsing under the thin skin of my swollen erection. Each time she swallowed it again,

I could feel the insides of her cheeks against the shaft.

I had never felt anything like it. I had never known such ecstasy was possible. I had never been so hard. Nothing had ever told me that my body was capable of achieving such heights. The sensations whirled and twirled like a tornado through my brain.

Instinctively, my hands reached for her head. I tangled my fingers in that gorgeous shock of thick red hair. It was soft and luxurious. I held on tightly, but I didn't control the movements of her head; I followed them.

She filled her throat with my cock, stopping only when her lips left their prints in my pubic hair. Then she pulled back, streaking the shaft with lipstick until only the head remained inside her mouth. She suckled it with bubbling movements of her lips before again sliding it deep beyond her tonsils.

Her hand rolled my balls around, coaxing the flow that was boiling inside me. I felt it starting to rise—that feeling of hot fluid tearing its way through my belly and all the way to its exit. I clutched tightly at her hair as the climax started to overtake me. Then I began to pump, and it just kept on going and going. I thought it would never stop. I didn't know how she could take it all, but she kept right on loving it.

When I was finished coming, my dick fell from her mouth. It was all over for her. I wasn't hard anymore. She had no further use for me. She wanted me gone. All of this came through to me without her saying a word. I just stood there, not knowing how to escape.

She got up without looking at me and walked to the side table in the hallway. "Here's a check for the groceries," she said, extending her arm. Quickly, I pulled up my pants, walked to the front door, took the check, and left. I hadn't said a single word the whole time I was there.

I never saw her again, because a few days later I went into the service, and by the time I got out, she had moved away. But I've thought about her ever since. There was something very strange about her and her weird world of penis worship. All I know is, whatever sort of exotic ritual she was performing, for me it was the best blow job I've ever had in my entire life. Maybe it's because it was my first time, and I was only nineteen. I don't know.

I'm not complaining about the other women I've known. They've all been good sex partners, and to me that means they've all been good at giving head. That will always be my favorite thing. But no one ever did it for me like the mystery lady.

IMAGINATION

We can't describe Lonnie because we have never met her face to face, just interviewed her on the phone after an exchange of computer E-mail. She wanted very much to tell us her story and to have us repeat it in our book. She seems quite worried about protecting her identity, however. All she will tell us about herself is that she is twenty-two. We have made up her name.

I like to think about oral sex. It really turns me on.

My husband has a tremendous sexual appetite. We usually have intercourse at least twice a day. On the weekends, when we don't have to go to work, we might have sex three or four times in a day.

Sometimes, we spend a long time at our lovemaking. We do everything to each other. I'm capable of multiple orgasms, and when he performs oral sex on me, I climax again and again. He's really very good at it.

He has a way of kissing my vagina so lightly and so gently that it feels like a breeze. Then he uses a little more pressure, and a little more, until his mouth is pressed tightly against me, sucking hard in all the right places.

He knows my genitals perfectly. He can lick tenderly at my clitoris until it almost reaches the point where I can't stand anymore. He'll know immediately and pull back just before it gets to be too much. Then he'll trail his tongue and lips so softly over the other sensitive parts of me that my clitoris starts begging for his attention again. He keeps it up until I have an orgasm and continues until I have another. Sometimes, I think if I didn't beg him to stop, he'd keep me coming forever.

But there are other times—especially before we leave for work in the morning—when we just have intercourse quickly, with no foreplay at all. I think men like to do it that way because it makes them feel like billy goats or stallions. I know my husband likes it. I enjoy it, too. I'm proud that my husband has such a hearty sexual appetite, and I like to know that I can satisfy it for him, that I can take all he wants to give and give all he wants to take.

I take a lot of pride in letting him do me whenever he feels like it. I hold myself open for him in whatever position he asks for, and I let him penetrate me for his own personal pleasure. I like letting him use my body for his needs, even though it doesn't usually bring me to orgasm.

Once in a while, I do have a climax while he's having his way with my body. Whenever that happens, it's because I've been thinking about oral sex. I close my eyes and imagine his tongue doing its work.

Sometimes, he has me lying on my back, and he mounts me missionary style. While he thrusts, I imagine that I'm lying in that same position with my legs spread wide as he licks me. I mentally compare the tenderness of his tongue with the massive thickness of his penis. While it fills me roughly, I think of his mouth making the smoothest possible contact. Other times I'm on my hands and knees for him while he enters me from behind. Then I think about times when he knelt behind me in that position, lapping at me with broad strokes of his tongue, until my orgasms flowed to make his face shine.

Maybe some other time, I'll have my ankles against his shoulders, feeling him driving in as deep as he possibly can. In that position, it almost feels as if his penis is too big for me to accept. While he parts the tissues of my vagina with his ramming thrusts, I picture his lips nibbling gently at my clitoris with the masterful finesse of an artist.

The mental images add to the sensations his penis is actually creating inside me, exciting me so much that I sometimes climax. It's like having him perform oral sex on me at the same time we're having intercourse.

He can always tell when I'm about to have an orgasm. I know it especially turns him on when it happens during one of our quick morning couplings. And that turns me on even more.

I've heard some women say that the only time they have orgasms is when they're having oral sex. In a way, the same is true for me. Only, sometimes, just thinking about oral sex is enough. Then I can come even during intercourse because the oral sex I'm having in my imagination turns me on.

LESSON

Manny looks and talks like a rough character, but is a very decent human being. He is small and wiry, having been toughened up on the streets of one of Chicago's meanest districts. He doesn't live in the old neighborhood anymore, but returns every day to work as a counselor in the local youth center. He says he knows how close he came as a kid to going bad and wants to help other kids get as lucky as he was. When he talks about sex, he smiles broadly, a wistfully nostalgic look coming into his dark flashing eyes.

I love going down on a woman. It's the greatest turn-on I know. Maybe that's because it's something I do really well. I owe all that to Amalia.

I grew up in a rotten neighborhood, in an old run-down building with exposed pipes and walls that sweated. Everybody who lived there was struggling to stay alive. Nobody looked down their nose at anybody else. Everybody knew that Amalia was a prostitute. In that neighborhood, there were lots of prostitutes. They weren't exactly thought of as pillars of the community, but we didn't spit on them either.

Amalia was different, though. Everybody loved and respected her. You might even say people looked up to her. Even though she peddled her ass for a living, she had the soul of a saint. She'd give you anything she had if she thought you needed it more than she did.

There was an old lady who lived down the hall. She needed dental surgery, but the welfare people said it was elective and turned her down. Amalia paid for it. Upstairs there was a fat lazy bastard who would leave his kids alone all day to go drinking while his wife was out working her ass off. Amalia always looked in on them and made sure they were fed. Her shoulder was always there for crying on when things got so bad you couldn't see any way out.

That's how I felt when I found myself still a virgin at the age of nineteen. The guys I ran with all made fun of me. Some of them had been getting laid regularly since they were twelve. Girls scared the shit out of me. I couldn't get anywhere with them. One day in desperation, I went to Amalia and asked her to let me lay her.

"I can't do that," she said, her voice soft with gentle sympathy. "You're my friend, and fucking is a business for me."

"I'll pay you," I offered. "I've got some money saved up."

"No, baby," she cooed. "Then we couldn't be friends no more. Why don't you get a regular girlfriend? You're a good-looking guy. You could get lots of girls. All's you need is a little confidence."

It sounded like bullshit to me, but I smiled bravely. "OK," I said sadly. "Sorry I asked." I was trying to hide my disappointment, but it must have shown.

"Tell you what," she said. "You come here tonight around two, when I'm finished working, and I'll show you how to please the girls so good that they'll all come running to you."

I glowed with gratitude. She was going to fuck me after all. I went home shaking all over and stayed that way well into the night. I showered and doused myself with the cheap cologne my mom gave me for Christmas. I wanted to smell good for Amalia.

I was at her door promptly at two A.M. At first, nothing happened when I knocked, and I thought she might have changed her mind or been delayed. I was about to walk away when I decided to try again. So I knocked once more, this time a little louder. I heard a chair scraping across the floor inside, and a moment later, Amalia opened the door to let me in.

"Come in and have some coffee," she said. "There's someone here I want you to meet." I was disappointed when I saw a young woman sitting at Amalia's kitchen table. I figured this would mean postponing our plans, and by then, maybe she'd change her mind.

I took the chair Amalia indicated and sat down as she poured me some coffee. "This is my friend, Teresa," she said, almost formally. "Teresa, this is Manny."

"How do you do?" I asked, reaching awkwardly across the table to shake Teresa's hand.

"Teresa's going to help me show you what I was talking about," Amalia explained, "just as soon as she finishes her coffee." Blood pounded in my temples as I wondered what she had in mind.

"The most important thing a man needs to know," she continued, "is how to eat pussy. If you can do that right, you'll be one in a million, and you'll never have a problem getting a girlfriend. 'Cause you'll have all the confidence you need."

A few minutes later, Teresa went to Amalia's bed, which was only a few steps away from the kitchen table. She took off her dress and lay on the bed, wearing nothing but a brief pair of black panties and a green satin bra. I was already excited beyond belief.

"No, no, no, Teresa," Amalia said. "Take everything off. I want to show Manny right." Without hesitation, Teresa sat up and removed the bra and panties, lying down again and spreading her legs. I stared in fascination at her naked snatch.

"Now, I suppose you know all about a woman's titties," Amalia began, sounding almost like the teachers I had when I was in school. "Some girls like you to touch their titties and suck on their nipples. You can figure that stuff out for yourself." As she spoke, she brushed her hand over Teresa's little breasts.

I wished I could be doing the same because I had never seen a woman's tits before, and the thought of touching Teresa's and sucking on them was exciting as hell. But Amalia went on. "I'm going to teach you about pussy," she said. "I'm going to show you all you need to know."

She sat next to Teresa and started giving me an anatomy lesson, touching each part as she talked. "This here's the clitty," she said, gently stroking the shining red button at the top of Teresa's slit. Teresa shuddered slightly at the contact. Amalia continued rubbing the tiny node. "See what I'm doing?" she asked. "It feels real nice for her, but you got to make sure it stays wet. Now put your finger inside and I'll show you a little trick."

I couldn't believe what was happening. This was really it. I was going to touch a woman's pussy for the first time in my life. My hand shook as I brought it closer. Tentatively, I inserted my middle finger between the soft feminine folds. The inside was hot and filled with thick moisture.

"See how wet she is?" Amalia asked. "Here's what you do. Take some of that juice and put it right here." She held Teresa's lips apart while I did as she instructed. "That's it," she said encouragingly. "Touch it real soft and easy. Spread it all around."

I was beside myself. I thought I was standing at the gates of heaven, but there was lots more in store. After Amalia directed my explorations of Teresa's clit, she led me through the same kind of exercise with every part of the other woman's genitals. My pants were damp from the excitement oozing out of me.

When she thought I understood the geography of a woman's sex, she pushed me gently back and said it was time for me to see how to use my tongue. While I watched, she brought her face close to Teresa's pussy and began performing oral sex on her. I could hardly breathe as I saw her tongue explore and penetrate every crease and crevice.

Teresa was obviously enjoying it, and the sounds she made seemed to inspire Amalia to do more things. I watched her going down on the other woman for several minutes, my eyes tracing every movement of her tongue and lips. Teresa was starting to moan even louder. I could tell something was going to happen. Before it did, Amalia stopped.

"See how good I been making her feel," she said. "Now you try it. I bet you can make her feel even better."

I didn't hesitate for a moment, throwing myself forward to taste the acrid flavor of Teresa's sex. I was awkward and clumsy at first, but it really didn't take long before I was eating her like I was born to it. I could tell by the way her body jerked in time to her moans. As I licked, I turned my head to look at Amalia, but she was busy sucking on Teresa's nipples, so I just went on exploring.

Then I noticed the flavor changing, and I heard Teresa shout. "Oh, yeah," she hollered. "Oh, do me. Do me hard." Her words made me hotter, and I buried my face in her. I kept lapping hungrily until I felt hands pushing me away.

"You got to stop now, baby," Amalia said proudly. "You made her come. You did real good. It was a sweet come for her. I know her, and I can tell." Then she looked at the front of my pants. "Looks like you had a good come, too," she said with a giggle. I followed her glance and saw a dark stain spreading over the cloth. I was soaking wet.

That night was like my confirmation. I was really a man. I had good reason to be confident. I had gotten a woman off. Not some naive little girl, either. This was a woman who had been around.

Amalia taught me well. Besides showing me what to do, she made me feel sure of myself. That was the most important thing of all. As she promised, once I learned how to perform oral sex on a woman, I never had trouble finding girlfriends. Sometimes, when I'm giving a woman the kind of loving I know how to give, I remember the oral sex lesson I got from Amalia and her friend.

11

SEX WITHOUT CONTACT

ALTHOUGH CIVILIZATION IS FREQUENTLY BLAMED FOR bringing pestilence and disease to more primitive societies, the spread of sexually transmitted disorders may represent a reversal of this process. Many historians believe that syphilis was first carried to Europe by crew members serving under Christopher Columbus, who contracted it while having intercourse with the primitives they encountered in the Western hemisphere. Some scientists have stated that AIDS probably originated in a relatively undeveloped region of central Africa, whence it spread to the entire world.

Once established, these diseases were communicated rapidly. Syphilis was a problem of epidemic proportions until the discovery of penicillin presented modern science with an effective weapon against it. So far, however, no one has found a cure for AIDS. The possibility of contracting this lethal disease is changing the sexual behavior of people in contemporary society, many of whom now recognize a need to take precautions against coming into contact with the virus that causes it.

As a result, a search is afoot for satisfying forms of safe sex. Masturbation is about as safe as any sexual activity can be, but it isn't always satisfying. Perhaps that is because, in designing sex as a system for reproduction, the Universal Architect equipped us with a predisposition to seek partners. Although most people find masturbation to be a reliable way of achieving orgasms, it is usually a solitary pursuit.

Some of the people we interviewed have found ways to turn autoeroticism into an activity for two or more. In this way, they are able to experience orgasm with a partner, yet without touching or being touched by another person. Not only do they find it satisfying, but many describe it as a favorite turn-on.

In addition to protecting against the hazard of contracting a deadly disease, no-contact sex is used by the people whose stories are told in this chapter as a way of avoiding other potential problems. Q-T-4-U is so nervous about the possibility of becoming involved in a sexually abusive relationship that she takes great care to remain unidentifiable while having telephone sex with nameless faceless strangers. Todd regards a thin pane of glass as a shield against the vulnerability he feels when achieving sexual release. Verna, Michael, and June use group masturbation as a way of deferring distracting intimate relationships until their educations are complete.

PHONE SEX

We met Q-T-4-U by computer and corresponded with her by E-mail for a while before we got together on the phone. When asked to describe herself, she says, "I look exactly like Marilyn Monroe." Then she laughs and adds, "Don't you know that on the computer and on the phone I can look like anyone I want? Or anyone you want?" She pauses for a moment and says, "Let's just say I'm twenty-six." Then she laughs again.

I've never actually had sex with anyone. Not in person, anyway. I was thinking about it once, but first I insisted that we both have HIV tests. And his came back positive!

Naturally, I dropped him like a hot potato. That experience terrified me so much that the thought of having actual contact with a man turns me off. I'm not going to expose myself to that risk. Ever! It's just too scary for me to think about.

I am human, however. I've got to have *some* relief, so I've been using modern technology to take care of that. I work as a systems analyst. Well, systems trainee, actually. Which means I'm not a full-fledged computer nerd yet, but I know my way around a logic board better than most people. I've got a pretty advanced setup at home, and I use it to access the BBS. Excuse me, that's what we call the computer bulletin boards.

You know what a computer bulletin board is, don't you? It's a way of linking computers together using telephone lines. It's a sophisticated electronic switchboard that lots of different computers can tie into. We use them to leave messages for each other by computer. We call those messages postings.

I'm talking about it as if there were actually a bulletin board hanging on a wall with people tacking little three-by-five cards on it, but it's really just blips of electricity coming together in an imaginary place somewhere out there in cyberspace, which is what we call the magical world where our computers talk to each other.

Well, what I mean is we talk to each other through our computers. Besides leaving public messages or sending private correspondence by E-mail, we can also have keyboard conversations in what we call "real time." That's where the words I type show up on your screen while I'm typing them, and you type an answer that shows up on my screen while you're typing it.

People use BBS to find others who share the same hobbies and interests. There's a BBS for every purpose. The ones I belong to are like electronic singles bars—cyber meat markets.

Some people who meet on the BBS actually end up getting together in person. You hear all the time about marriages that start out as bulletin board romances, but I'm not interested in anything like that. I just surf the BBS for phone sex partners. There are lots of horny people out there looking for the same. Fortunately for me, most of them are men, so I really have my choice about who I connect with. Not that you can tell much about a person from what he posts to the bulletin board. Most people don't even use their own names. They have user IDs. Mine is Q-T-4-U. Like I said, on a computer, you can be anybody you want. Maybe that's one of the reasons it turns me on so much.

Typically, a BBS posting is only a few lines. It might say something like, "I'm looking for a sexy lady for hot conversations." Or, "Female phone partner wanted for exchange of fantasies."

Sometimes, people get pretty specific about what kind of fantasies they want to talk about. Some guys let you know they are into spanking scenes, or they want to reminisce about sexual experiences from childhood. Others get off on anal sex. There's a whole plethora of perversions. I've tried them all!

Some of the guys leave E-mail addresses, so you can get to know each other by exchanging computer messages. I never answer those postings, because it seems to me that they're trying to start some kind of cyber-relationship, and I don't want any relationship at all. Some are looking for real time conversations by keyboard. I tried that, but it didn't work out so well. I like to have both hands free for other things.

Now, I just look for the ones who post their phone numbers. Some of these guys have 800 numbers, so I could call for free, but my number would show up on his bill next month, and I'm not giving my number out to anyone. I don't call collect either, for the same reason, even though lots of men post messages saying they'll accept collect calls.

Paying for the call myself is a cheap price to pay for security. I even protect myself against caller ID machines by punching in star-six-seven before I make the call. That way, if they do have caller ID, their equipment won't be able to get my number.

Maybe it sounds like dry-tech, but to me everything about it is extremely exciting: logging on to the BBS, looking through the postings, picking one out, selecting a backup just in case the first one isn't in, writing down the numbers. What I'm doing is finding an absolute stranger to have an orgasm with, wondering all the while what my phone sex partner is going to be like. Every step turns me on a little more.

I usually go into the bedroom and take all my clothes off before I make the call. I use the speaker phone on my nightstand so I can stretch out comfortably on the bed. If his posting tells me what he's looking for, I think up an identity to go with the fantasy. Otherwise, I am whoever I feel like being that night. As soon as I finish dialing, I lay back and start stroking myself. I'm already all turned on, just by the idea of what I'm doing.

When his phone rings, he doesn't know who's calling. Maybe it's his mother, or somebody trying to sell him a subscription. So I usually get just an ordinary hello. Then, in a sexy voice, I say, "Is this Buck?" or whatever his user ID is.

When he hears that, he knows what the call is going to be about. I just love to hear his sound of excited surprise. All men are different, but in that way they're all the same. When the hormones start flowing, something happens to the voice. I can recognize it every time.

I don't want to spend any time getting to know him. I like the idea that he's a total stranger, and I want to keep it that way. That's part of the turn-on.

So I usually start right in. "I'm naked," I might whisper, "and my pussy is itching for you." I really like to talk dirty, as long as I'm sure the guy won't ever know who I am.

I ask him to undress and to describe his cock to me. Or maybe I *order* him to do it, depending who or what I've decided to be. They're all sixteen inches long and as thick as a baseball bat, of course. Remember, you can be anybody you want.

That's another part of the turn-on. I mean, how many women ever get a guy with a cock as big as that. If they do, it's liable to kill them. But when he puts it in me over the phone, no matter how big it is, it doesn't hurt. Unless I'd like it to, that is. 'Cause if I do, it'll hurt exactly as much as I want.

They always want a description of my tits. I like that part. Sometimes I'm a 44D, with big red nipples like ripe strawberries. Sometimes I've got little A-cup cuties that just about make a mouthful.

The only thing we really know about each other is that we're doing ourselves like crazy while all this conversation is going on. We might talk openly about the stroking. I'll tell him exactly what I'm doing with my fingers, and he'll tell me the same. Or maybe we don't even mention it. Instead, we describe the exotic sex acts we're performing on each other. But you can be sure those hands are working the whole time.

You get to be an expert after a while on breath sounds and what they mean. I can always tell when the guy is about to get his rocks off. I try to work things out so that we come simultaneously. It's more exciting that way.

Then, when I'm finished with myself, I'm finished with him. If I feel like it, I say good-bye. Otherwise, I just hang up. Why not? I won't be talking to him again. No need to. There are hundreds of them out there. I might as well try them all. You see, that way I get to have sex with a different guy every time.

It's the safest sex around because we have absolutely no contact with each other, no chance of disease, no chance of getting involved with an abusive partner. Those are the real reasons I do it. Also, it just happens to be the best turn-on I know. At least for now.

PEEP SHOW

Todd, twenty-eight, proudly announces that his family has been in the landscape business for three generations, ever since his grandfather immigrated from Portugal. He is about 5'9", with broad shoulders and a slim waist. His swarthy complexion is darkened by hours spent in the sun laying out jobs and supervising his workers. His dark hair and beard contrast with his pale blue eyes to add a Rasputin-like look of sinister mystery to his overall appearance.

Irina and I have been living together for a little over a year now. Some day we might get married, but for now we're perfectly content to share our lives without the approval of the civil authorities. We have a good life, a good sex life, too. You know, I read books about people who have sex a hundred times a day, but it's not that way for us. Our sex is always great, but twice a week is usually enough. It's not that our schedules prevent it. I usually get home by five-thirty and most of the time she's already there. It's just that neither of us wants it more than that.

There is one kind of sex, though, that I could have fifty times a week. It's perfectly safe, and Irina even knows about it. It's sex through a pane of glass. I call it no-contact sex. Nothing—not a thing in the whole wide world—turns me on the way that does. I don't know why. Maybe you can figure it out.

There's a place in town called the Gents Room. I discovered it one day while driving to a job where we were setting up a tea garden in an office building. The sign said LIVE NUDE GIRLS, and I just had to stop. I never could resist the sight of live nude girls.

Inside it looked like an ordinary porno shop, where they sell sex toys like vibrators, and inflatable sex dolls, dirty books, and videos. I didn't see any live nude girls. The person behind the counter was fully dressed. Besides, he was an elderly man, at least seventy. I heard music blasting and realized there was some kind of an arcade in back. When I started to walk back there, the old guy said I had to buy two dollars' worth of tokens, so I did.

The arcade had a series of little booths grouped in a semicircle and connected to each other. I walked over to investigate and stepped inside one of the booths. It was tiny, and when I closed the door behind me, it was almost totally dark. On the wall in front of me was a glass window, maybe two feet square, and next to it a slot illuminated by a green LED light.

I dropped a token in the slot but nothing happened. I dropped in another and another. After a dollar's worth, a black curtain on the other side of the glass window opened. Now I could see a stage, small but brightly lit. Directly behind it were mirrors, and in them I could see reflections of the rest of the booths. A few of the curtains were open like mine, but a trick of the light made it impossible to see inside them.

I could see the live nude girls just fine, though. There were four of them on the stage, totally undressed and gyrating to the blaring sounds of rock and roll. Three were facing me, but the fourth was standing right in front of the window of another booth. The stage was elevated, so the bottom of the window started just above her knees. I could see her back and her ass reflected in the mirrors behind the stage, but only the guy in the booth could see the front of her. Her body was pressed tight against the glass, and I imagined her breasts squashed flat before his eyes.

I was wondering what I had to do to get into his shoes, or into that booth anyway, when one of the girls on stage looked in my direction and said, "Would you like a close-up?" She appeared Latin—Mexican, maybe, or Central American. And young, not much more than twenty. Her breasts were firm and pointy, but not very big. She had a real thick mat down below, and I've always liked that. Not exactly a beauty, but sexy and cute.

A "close-up," she called it. That was what I wanted, all right. A close-up.

She gestured toward a little opening at the top of the window, and I got the idea right away. I fumbled in my pocket and brought out a five-dollar bill. When I held it up to the glass to ask if it was enough, she came right over and reached toward the slot. I slipped the bill through the opening, and she took it from my hand.

Without wasting a second, she turned around and bent over to press her bottom against the window. Her cheeks spread as she flattened them against the glass, framing her open sex right there in front of me. The feeling I got was completely out of sight.

This was as close as a man could ever get to a woman's vagina without actually touching or entering it. The glass was all that separated us. It was barely a quarter of an inch thick and it was transparent, but it might as well have been a concrete barricade. I could look all I wanted, but no way could I touch. That made it very exciting. I could put my face, my eyes, my mouth right next to her, but I didn't have to do a thing. This was all for me and for me alone. I was very hard.

She turned around and knelt on the stage, so that the top half of her body was in front of the glass. She smiled at me and licked her lips, cupping her breasts in her hands as though offering them to me. "I'm Honey," she said, "and I'm here from nine to six every day. Enjoy. There are paper towels to your right."

I thought about the paper towels and realized they were an invitation to masturbate. It seemed like a very healthy idea. It may sound strange to say it, but compared to some of the other things you hear about, this is good clean fun.

The young lady flattened her breasts against the glass, centering each little rock hard bud of a nipple in a circle of smooth tan skin. I cupped one by placing my hand on the glass. A little self-consciously, I used my other hand to reach down and unzip my pants.

I extracted my penis and started stroking it as she stood up in front of the glass. There must have been a rail or a ledge on her side of the wall because she lifted one foot high and perched it next to the window so that she was standing on one leg with her sex pulled wide open right there in front of me.

Believe it or not, I once saw an orchid so erotic that it gave me an erection. I remembered it as I stood staring in silence at the subtle pinks and reds of her labia. I don't think I ever realized before how beautiful a woman's sex organ is.

There must be a nerve that runs straight from my eyes to my penis because the sight of her spread open for me made it swell even more. I kept stroking it all the while, sometimes lightly and sometimes roughly. It gave me a feeling I never had before.

It was so weird. She didn't know me at all, and all I knew about her was that fake name, Honey. But she was willing to show me her private parts for just a few dollars, and she knew that I was jacking off while she showed them to me. The thought gave me a perverted kind of kick.

At first, I didn't think I would go all the way. Masturbation is a very private thing. A man loses control of himself when he ejaculates. He is never more vulnerable than that very moment. That's why we are only supposed to have sex with someone we love and trust and feel closest to. But the glass window was there to protect me. It made it safe for me to be vulnerable with this pretty young stranger. When my climax began, I think it was the freest feeling I had ever known. I just let myself go, spewing into infinity.

Somehow she knew when I was done, and she did something on her side of the wall to make the black curtain come down. Just as the booth was plunged into darkness again, I heard her say, "Remember Honey."

I rearranged my clothing before opening the door and stepping into the real world again. There was a bit of a shock in coming out into a lighted room where men were walking around looking relatively normal. When I got back into my car, I glanced at my watch and realized I had been in the place less than fifteen minutes. Funny, it had felt like a lifetime.

I thought about it as I drove home after work. When I got there, I was all excited again. Much more than usual, in fact. Irina and I had a pretty hot time. Later, she asked what made me come home in such a state, and I told her all about it. I thought she might be angry, but she said she liked the idea.

Now, she sometimes calls me at work to suggest that I stop off at the Gents Room on the way home. I always know that means that she's in the mood for some special loving. She knows my no-contact sex is going to turn me on, and that works out nicely for both of us.

HOUSEMATES

Verna is not quite twenty-one, with skin the color of coffee and black hair cropped close to her head. Her round chocolate eyes are deep and expressive. She is 5'4" and just a little on the plump side. In an open and unabashed way, she describes her favorite erotic activity.

It's sex without touching. We started doing it because it was the only safe, sane, and sensible way of fulfilling our needs, but it's turned out to be such a turn-on that I can't imagine living without it.

I've always been serious about my education. When I was in high school, I looked forward to college, not because of the social life, but because of the classes I would get to take. I had done a little dating and even had sex a few times with a boy I thought I was serious with, but it was just a teenage romance.

When I started college, I decided that I wouldn't get involved with anybody until I had my degree. Now I'm just a year away from it. June and Michael feel the same way. They're my housemates and my very best friends. We didn't even know each other until we started college and Roommate Search brought us together. That was almost three years ago. We've been sharing this house ever since.

All three of us study hard. June goes out on dates once in a while, but just as a social thing and not usually twice with the same guy. She's very attractive. Her long blond hair and movie-star figure attract lots of male attention, so she could have plenty of men if she wanted them. But she says she'll have time for relationships later. Now, she's got exams to take.

Michael isn't bad looking either, in an intense scholarly way. He's a math major, and when he's concentrating on a problem, his forehead furrows and his dark bushy eyebrows move closer to each other until they're almost touching. It makes him look brilliant. I've seen women stare at him with open hunger. He, also, has made a conscious decision to postpone courtship and dating until he gets his degree.

At our age, we should be at the peak of sexual activity. Our hormones are running absolutely wild. I guess that's why we all use masturbation as an outlet.

Of course, at first, I didn't realize the others were doing it. I thought I was the only one. Some nights, when I had been studying until my eyes burned, I would lie awake in bed fingering myself. Usually, I would climax within three or four minutes and then drift off to sleep. It felt good, but I did it more for relief than for pleasure.

Then one night, I made an interesting discovery. I was having a problem with my statistical analysis class and thought I would ask Michael for help with it. I didn't want to disturb his studies, however, so I approached his room quietly, thinking I'd just peek in and see whether he was free.

His door was slightly open—just a crack. I don't think he even knew it. He was sitting at his desk, but his chair was pulled back and his pants and underpants were down around his ankles. He had a huge erection and was stroking it up and down with his hand. I had never seen him with his clothes off, and I was surprised at how big he was.

I stood there fascinated, my eyes riveted to the sight of his organ. I watched him increase the speed of his hand movements and heard him moan softly as he started to spurt. Grabbing a Kleenex, he clapped it over the end of his penis to catch the ejaculate. After that, all I could see were the spasmodic movements of his body as the tissue darkened with moisture. His eyes were tightly closed, but I knew he would open them as soon as his orgasm finished.

I was horribly ashamed and terrified that he might catch me peeping at him. I ran back to my room on tiptoes, a blush warming my cheeks. My face wasn't the only thing getting hot. I felt a burning desire between my legs. I threw myself into bed and buried my fingers in my vagina. My head spun with images of what I had witnessed. I climaxed almost immediately, picturing the size of Michael's erection. It filled my imagination as tremors of orgasm flooded my body with a sense of relief.

The next morning, I felt guilty about having spied on Michael. I decided the only way to atone for my sin was to make a full confession. I waited until I heard him moving around in the kitchen. Then, slipping into sweats, I joined him. He was in pajamas. I poured myself a cup of the coffee he had just brewed. We both sat at the table, sipping it and eating cereal with milk.

Finally, I said, "Michael, I hope you'll forgive me, but I watched you last night." He looked at me, puzzled, and I thought I needed to give further explanation. "I was coming in to ask you for help with something and I caught you masturbating. I know I should have walked away, but I stayed there, watching until you were all done. I want to apologize."

Michael's face took on a faraway smile. "I thought I felt a presence," he said, "but I wasn't sure." He seemed to be thinking for a moment before adding, "That was a dirty trick, but I'll accept your apology if you tell me how you felt while you were watching me."

"I'll admit it turned me on," I said, staring down into my cereal bowl to avoid meeting his eyes. "Right afterwards, I went to my own room and masturbated, too."

"Describe it to me," he said. "Tell me all about it."

I felt a flush of embarrassment. "Don't ask me to do that," I pleaded. "I just couldn't."

"All right," he said. "I can understand that. Then how about showing me."

I was astonished. "You're kidding, aren't you?" I stammered.

"No, not really," he answered. "You watched me. It's only fair that I get to watch you. Besides, it turned you on. I know it would turn me on, too. I'm getting turned on just talking about it. Just let me see it. I promise I won't try to touch you or anything like that."

On impulse, I said, "I'll do it. I'll let you see everything, but only if you let me watch you at the same time." I was shocked to hear the words coming out of my mouth and even more shocked a moment later when I found myself on the couch in the living room getting ready to actually go through with it.

Michael sat in the easy chair on the other side of the room. For a moment we were both silent. Then he stood and, without a word, took off his pajama bottoms. Following his lead, I removed my sweats, top and bottom.

There was something indescribably sexy about sitting there in the nude. I saw him looking at my breasts and felt my nipples become hard. He was obviously aroused by the sight of me because his penis was jumping to full erection.

He started pumping it up and down, staring at me all the while. I watched him and felt myself becoming incredibly aroused. Then, aware that he could see everything I did, I began caressing my breasts and nipples. I didn't usually do that when I masturbated alone, but having him watch me that way inspired me. I kept petting my breasts with one hand while I started stroking my genitals with the other.

We were both so involved that we jumped when we heard June's voice. "What a great idea," she said. She had apparently been watching us for some time. "Mind if I join?"

Michael and I had been so preoccupied with ourselves that we forgot about June, who was sleeping in her room on the other side of the living room wall. I was so embarrassed, I couldn't speak. But Michael answered her, "Please do."

June was wearing a long sleep shirt, and I could see her hard nipples poking against it. Michael and I stared at her as she bent down to take the hem in her hands. With a single efficient movement, she straightened up and pulled it over her head. Her breasts were full and round, with huge pink nipples. A mass of golden hair grew wild all over the bottom of her belly and the tops of her thighs.

She threw a cushion down on the floor and sat on it with her knees apart, so Michael and I would have an unobstructed view of her genitals. I had never looked at another female that way, at least not since I was five or six years old. Her vulva was beautiful, and I found my gaze moving from her to Michael and back again, as all three of us began masturbating.

I felt a childlike sense of discovery. I had known that everyone masturbated, of course, but I had never thought about the details. June did things to herself that I had never tried. Probably I was doing things that were new to her. We watched each other, learning new techniques for self-gratification as we went along. Michael's hand was flying up and down as he looked from one of us to the other.

The best part was seeing their orgasms, seeing the way their faces contorted when their satisfaction arrived. When I came, there was extra pleasure in knowing I was being watched.

Afterwards, the three of us sat together in silence, none of us knowing what to say or do next. Finally, Michael put his pajama pants back on and said, "That was totally excellent. I'd sure like to do this again, but now I've got studying to do."

We did do it again that night and many nights thereafter. It has become our regular sexual outlet. It's got a lot going for it. For one thing, we don't get involved in distracting relationships. For another, it's totally safe, absolutely disease-free. We tell that to each other all the time. Maybe it's a way of excusing our behavior, but the honest truth is, it simply turns us on.

CONCLUSION

THE MOST IMPORTANT MESSAGE THIS BOOK OFFERS IS THAT the things that turn people on are as different as people themselves. We have included some common turn-ons, like romance and touching. We have also included some uncommon ones, like being watched or having sex without contact. Upon reflection, however, the only thing common or uncommon about the stories our informants gave us is the extent to which they carried out the activities involved.

Take the chapter on sex talk, for example. Almost everyone finds it arousing to talk about sex. During foreplay, some whisper, "Touch me there." At the moment of orgasm, some shout, "Oh, it feels so good." We humans are vocal animals, and it is natural for the use of language to play some role in our sexuality.

Few go so far as to discuss with their mates in intimate detail the acts they performed with extramarital paramours. At first glance, this makes Ray and Surya's bar game seem outlandish and aberrant. But if the essence of their turn-on is talk, the difference is just a matter of degree.

Similarly, not many people are willing to permit others to watch them having intercourse. This makes Millie and Jeff's participation in sex research, and the same-room sex parties of Amber and Ivan, appear unusual and extreme. Again, however, the only real difference between their form of exhibitionism and the more common varieties is the length to which they go.

Lots of us like showing off. If we didn't, the manufacturers of bikinis and tank T-shirts would be casting about for other products to sell. No honest and introspective person can deny that at least some of the pleasure associated with this rather mild form of display is linked to sexuality. Once that admission is made, it is only a short step to see the connection between a plunging neckline and making love before an audience.

This is not to suggest that if you like to wear revealing garments, you should invite strangers into your bedroom. Or that if you and your mate whisper during sex, you should start telling each other about erotic acts you performed with others. No two people or couples are the same. The spice that seasons one relationship might poison another. What we are trying to say is that when we open our minds, we usually find that the gulfs between us are not as wide as they appear. Realizing this makes it easier to understand other people. In turn, that makes it easier to understand ourselves.

This book is about what turns people on. There are a number of ways to read and use it. At its most basic level, reading the explicit descriptions that some of the people we interviewed were willing to give may be an erotic stimulant. This book may become one of the things that turns *you* on.

By presenting a peek into the bedrooms and minds of other members of our species, this book may also furnish an insight into the human condition. Remember, aside from the fact that they were willing to talk to us about their sex lives, there is nothing distinctive about any of the people whose stories we have told. They are librarians and landscapers and truck drivers and students, just like the rest of us. One of them may be living on your street.

Undoubtedly, there are some people on your street who do things in private that you never imagined. If, initially, that strikes you as a scary thought, think about the people and activities described in this book. Strange as some of their practices may seem, the people aren't scary at all. In addition, most of their practices are related, in kind if not extent, to some of our own. Recognizing that connection may help us all to better understand ourselves.

When you read about other people's favorite turn-ons, you probably find something exciting in each of them. We know we do. When you think about your own favorite turn-ons, you will probably find that, to some extent, they bear resemblance to activities described in this book. If not, we'd like to hear about it.

ATTENTION
READERS

THE AUTHORS HAVE ALREADY BEGUN GATHERING INFORMA-tion for their next book. If you would like to participate by filling out a questionnaire, please get in touch with:

Iris and Steven Finz
P.O. Box 237
The Sea Ranch, CA 95497
E-mail: huck@mcn.org